the Breast Book

PORTOBELLO
ROAD W11
One way

the Breast Book

A puberty guide with a difference – it's the when, why and how of breasts

Emma Pickett

The Breast Book: A puberty guide with a difference – it's the when, why and how of breasts

First published by Pinter & Martin Ltd 2019

ISBN 978-1-78066-475-0

Also available as an ebook

Editor: Susan Last
Index: Helen Bilton
Cover Design: Blok Graphic, London
Illustrations: Fontaine Anderson
Photographs: RÅN studio

British Library Cataloguing-in-Publication Data
A catalogue record for this book is available from the British Library.

Set in Linoletter Std and ITC American Typewriter
Printed and bound in the EU by Hussar

This book has been printed on paper that is sourced and harvested from sustainable forests and is FSC accredited.

Pinter & Martin Ltd
6 Effra Parade
London SW2 1PS

pinterandmartin.com

Previous page: Photography by © RÅN studio

Contents

happybirthday

Introduction

Are you at the age when everyone keeps saying, *'Aren't you getting big? Aren't you getting tall? Aren't you growing up?'*

People have been doing that since you were teeny tiny, and your parents have been hearing it for years. When you were not much bigger than a loaf of bread, people still said you were 'big'. When you could finally stretch up and reach a door handle, they got really excited. When you smooshed a vegetable near your mouth for the first time and when you walked, people jumped up and down.

You've been constantly changing for a long time. You've been changing on the inside and on the outside and now hormones are coming along which are getting you ready to be an adult in new ways.

When breasts first start to grow, it doesn't normally get talked about. The family friend or your auntie who said, 'Aren't you getting tall?' is not about to say, 'Look! Your breasts are arriving!'. It's not what people do.

You get a birthday card when you are 10 and that's just about planet Earth going around the sun 10 times, but there aren't any greetings cards that say, 'Congratulations on the appearance of your breasts!'

And why do grannies give book vouchers and not bra vouchers?

It's natural to feel a bit embarrassed talking about our body changing. I'm not saying it's WRONG that your friend didn't have her last birthday party with a 'Woo Hoo! We're going to get breasts!' theme and there wasn't a bra in the party bag when you went home. (The cake would have looked interesting).

When our bodies change, it's normal to want to feel a bit more private about things. It's not always easy to talk about changing, but sometimes we find ourselves worrying and wishing we could talk to someone, while at the same time not really wanting to. It can be confusing.

Perhaps someone bought you this book as a present and that was embarrassing. Maybe they said, 'And if you have any questions…' and you felt yourself die inside at the thought of THAT conversation.

That's perfectly normal, but some of our embarrassment talking about breasts doesn't come from a good place. We sometimes feel embarrassed because the way we talk about breasts in our society is mixed up.

We live in a society that isn't quite sure how to talk about breasts. They *seem* to be important in lots of ways, but there are all these rules that say when we are allowed to talk about them and when we're not, and when we're allowed to show them and when we're not.

Who gets to decide all these rules? When you are 10 or 11, it can feel like you don't have much say in the matter. We'll talk about the 'rules' and also talk about the fact that YOU are the one who really gets to decide what goes when it comes to your breasts. You will make the rules for yourself and for your daughters.

By the end of this book, I want you to know all about breasts and feel confident about their arrival. I want you to understand how your body is changing and how other women have felt about those changes. Breasts are important. They are cool and work in clever ways. Scientists don't truly understand all the things they can do.

Many years from now, you may have a baby and it's going to need feeding. You may also have cousins and sisters and mums and friends who are having babies right now. Knowing what they are going through and feeling comfortable with the fact that feeding a baby is part of their lives is going to help everyone. One day, it might even help you.

We're called mammals because we give our babies milk that we make ourselves. The proper name for breasts is 'mammary glands'. In science lessons, teachers talk about mammals having hair and 'giving birth to live young', but it's the breasts and milk-making that really define us. Mammals can look very different – elephants, bats, cows, tigers, dolphins, Beyoncé. We're all mammals. We all make milk. Beyoncé did it for her twin babies. Opossums can do it for 27 babies at once!

Whales have mammary glands that weigh as much as a baby elephant. There's a bat the size of a bumblebee that lives in Thailand. Think what size that bat's breasts must be – and their babies!

Some mums don't choose to breastfeed or find it difficult and we'll talk about that too. Some women find having breasts a bit tricky – even when babies aren't attached. But lots of women feel that breasts deserve a celebration.

We will say a bit of a 'woo hoo!' for breasts.

Message for parents/carers

There are lots of books about growing-up and puberty. This one is a bit different. It's not trying to cover the multitude of different topics that some do – but just one (or should that be two?).

For many women in the UK, the first time they reflect on what their breasts were created for is in the few months between discovering they are pregnant and when the baby is born. We spend a lifetime considering breasts as either to do with sexual attraction, or not a subject to discuss at all. Then suddenly, when preparing for motherhood, women are bombarded with information and told to rethink all their previous assumptions about breasts. That can be overwhelming and has led to a society with some of the lowest breastfeeding rates in human history.

This book doesn't suggest breastfeeding is the only option. It discusses women who either couldn't breastfeed or chose not to. However, chances are that if you are in the UK, either you or your partner didn't breastfeed for as long as you wanted to. We know about 80% of mothers wish they could have breastfed for longer. That can be about people not getting the support they need and a culture that isn't always comfortable talking about breastfeeding, including some of the basics of how it works.

This book aims to make breasts and breastfeeding normal. It sows a few seeds that may not be needed again for many years and meanwhile helps the women around us with their new babies – the ones in coffee shops, our sisters and our friends. Most young girls around the world, and through human history, have grown up seeing breastfeeding all around them. It's not even something they've noticed, it's just what your mum's friend does as she sips her tea and chats to you about your day. Girls absorb information on how to hold babies, how babies behave and how feeding babies is part of normal life. For them, breasts aren't about sex and being sexy – they are useful. Our girls deserve a piece of that.

Aside from a discussion on breastfeeding, it's a chance to talk about some other issues. How do breasts arrive? Is it OK if I don't look like my friend? Why do people buy bras and when? How do women feel about having breasts? How can social media and advertising impact on how we feel about our bodies?

Our girls will be growing up in a world full of selfies and videos and Snapchat and online discussions that make old-fashioned worries about magazine covers and billboard advertising pale in comparison. Tween and early teen girls aren't too young to understand that they are in control of their images and that messages from others aren't always helpful. Understanding how the commercial world aims to push them around isn't a conversation that can start too young.

This book also contains the story of Jack who grew up having breasts but is trans and now identifies as a he. In the 21st century, it feels like we should be ready to hear his story at this age. However, this may be something you want to talk about with the owner of the book before they read this section on their own.

Girls experience changes at different times and one 9 or 10-year-old can look very different from another. They may also be ready to look at the world in different ways at different ages. For some, this book will be right at around 10 years old, while for others it will be a better fit at around 12 or 13.

CHAPTER ONE

Being a teeny baby

Once upon a time you were a bundle of cells inside your mum. You were smaller than a grain of rice. You were made from an egg cell and a sperm cell. They joined together and life began. Then you grabbed onto the lining of your mum's womb and got stuck in and that's where you stayed for about 40 weeks.

Your mum fed you through the umbilical cord that connected you. When she ate sandwiches, they were broken down into their nutritional components, which floated through her bloodstream and through the cord and were the building blocks that helped you to grow. You were sandwiches and roast dinners and chocolate and apples. You were curries and sausages and vitamin pills and biscuits. You didn't need to eat any food yourself because you had a delivery system that was perfectly designed. Your mum's body was able to break her food down into all its important parts. She got some and you got some too. You took calcium for your bones and protein to make your muscles. You needed iron for your blood and fats to grow your brain.

Nature is clever. Nature is so clever that even when you were being built out of sandwiches, it was getting you ready for the time you might one day be a parent. As you were

Embryo at four weeks

Embryo at six weeks

Foetus at nine weeks

floating around in the special fluid inside your mum's womb, your breasts were just starting out. When you were smaller than a pea (4–6 weeks), your breasts were already beginning to grow! That's before you even had feet.

In fact, breasts are so important to human development that everyone gets them at the start, even if they don't end up being a woman! You've probably noticed that boys have nipples too. Boys and men have nipples because every baby starts out making breasts just in case. Then after about six weeks, hormones come along that give messages to the boy's body to stop making breasts and worry about other things instead and girls' bodies carry on working on the breasts. Hormones are special chemicals that send messages around the body and switch things on and off. They tell your body which bits to grow and help lots of systems to work properly. Women have hormones called oestrogen and progesterone that help their body make breasts.

While your mum was pregnant, her tummy was getting bigger, but hormones meant her breasts were too. Her breasts were beginning to make milk weeks before you arrived. Her nipples and areola (the coloured circle around the nipple) changed so you'd be able to use them more easily. Some mums even notice they start leaking milk weeks and weeks before it's time for the baby to come out.

Inside grown-up breasts, there are some fatty bits. Those are the bits that wobble when someone runs around. A mesh of ligaments called Cooper's ligaments support the whole breast against the muscle on the chest wall. Lobes, lobules and alveoli are the parts that make milk. Alveoli bunch together like tiny grapes to make lobes. The grapes are where the milk is made. The stalks that join the grapes together are like the milk ducts where the milk flows down towards the baby. The ducts finish at the surface of the skin around the nipple.

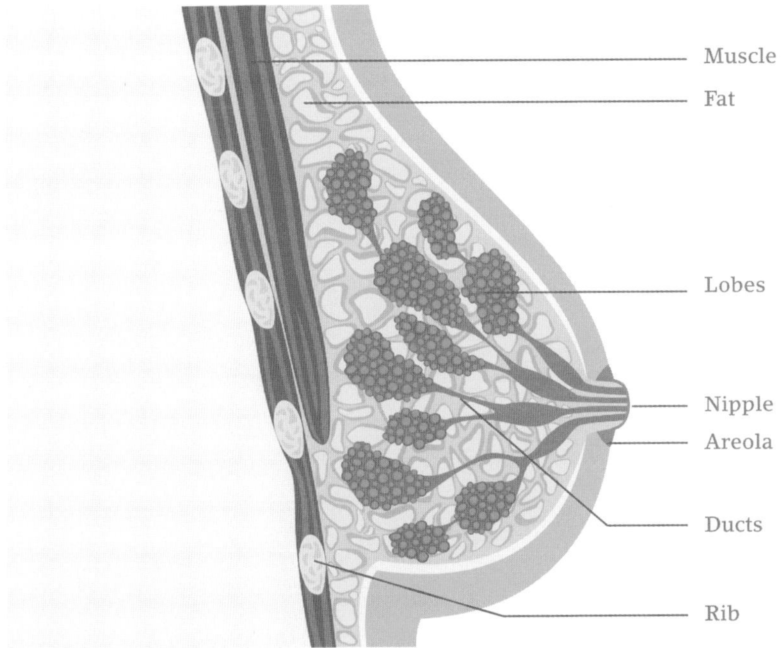

When your mum was pregnant, her hormones woke up the milk-making parts inside her breast and they did some extra growing. Some of the milk-making bits had started to get ready when she was a child, and they grew more when she was a teenager, but it was only when she was pregnant with you that her body really said, 'OK! Come on! It's milk time!'.

Then you are born. You're on a mission to be as close to your mum as you can be. You've been inside for nine months where it was warm and comfy and had soothing noises like your mum's heart beat and her voice. The minute you are out, the outside world is cold and bright and loud and scary.

You want to stick close. Usually when babies are born, they are placed on mum's chest and do their first feed at the breast within an hour of birth. Even when no one helps them, they will often wiggle their way to mum's breasts all by themselves – that's how desperately they want to be there.

The first milk is called colostrum and it's special milk designed just for brand-new babies that lasts a few days before the regular milk arrives. It is packed full of germ-fighting ingredients and helps protect a baby before all the germs in the big wide world try and muscle in on the scene.

You might think that milk always looks white. What kind of milk have you spent most of your life looking at? I'm guessing it's probably cow's milk. It looks white because of the amount of fats and proteins that little cows need

"The first milk is called colostrum and it's special milk designed just for brand-new babies."

and it's also been homogenised. That means it has been processed in a machine so the fat molecules have broken down into tiny bits that will always stay spread out in the liquid. It's white because it reflects the light around it. Fats and proteins are really good at reflecting light.

Human milk is a bit different. That first milk called colostrum is a yellow golden colour. As a mum's milk starts to change, it gets paler and whiter. Sometimes it looks quite watery even though it's got exactly the right amount of fat that a baby needs. Later on, it might even look a bit blue or even a bit green!

Humans don't need much fat compared to other animals. A whale makes milk that is about one-third pure fat. A grey seal makes milk that is more than half pure fat. Human milk has only a tiny fraction of that amount.

Think about how grey seals live their lives. They live in very cold seas – some of the coldest on the planet. They sleep on windy rocks. They need a layer of fat to keep themselves alive in harsh conditions. When a little baby seal arrives, it needs to start putting on fat FAST. When a baby cow arrives, it's going to have big strong muscles and in quite a short time it can start having its own babies, so cow's milk contains more protein to build muscles than human milk. We don't need to worry about sleeping on cold rocks or running around fields and having babies for ages. Cows can start having babies when they are TWO. What were you doing when you were two? Probably just starting to practise mooing like a cow! And no offence cows, but they are not the most intelligent animals on the planet. Our brains have a lot of developing to do.

Our brains are big compared to other animals. We also walk around on two legs, which means our hip bones have to be able to support us standing up. It's not easy giving birth to a child with such a big head and pushing it out through the space between the upright hip bones, so nature organises a clever system. We give birth to babies when they are quite undeveloped. Unlike baby horses, which can stand up and run around a field just a short time after giving birth, we're really just blobs. Very beautiful and wonderful blobs, but compared to other members of the animal kingdom, baby humans are not exactly advanced. It means pregnant mums can push the baby's head out without too much trouble and birth goes OK. But it also means human babies need a lot of looking after. Cow babies can be mums themselves when they are just two years old. Tigers can be mums when they are three or four. Gorillas can be mums when they are about seven. That's still a loooong time before humans are ready.

Our brain has a lot of growing to do as soon as we are born. And we are small and vulnerable. We need to stick with our parents because we're not much use by ourselves. At two years old, we might be able to make a mooing sound, but we can't find our own food (discovering an old raisin down the back of the sofa doesn't count). We need someone else to feed us and to keep us warm and safe. Our parents can't leave us for much time at all. Rabbit mums leave their babies in a nest while they go off and look for food. Instead, we are hoping to be carried around like gorilla mums carry their babies. Like gorillas and monkeys, we are primates. Our milk has just what we need to form clever and complex brains.

Because we are born early so that our big brains can squeeze out of our mums without causing too much trouble, our ability to fight disease – our immune system – needs some extra help.

When you are a baby and you or your mum come into contact with a germ that causes a disease, your mum's body does something amazing. It makes antibodies, special germ-fighting ingredients, that go into her milk to fight off that disease and reduce the chances you will get ill.

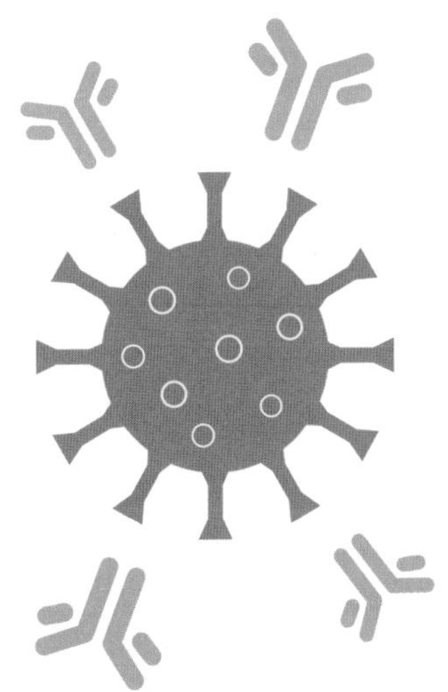

If someone sneezes on your pram on the bus, your mum's breastmilk soldiers will get to work. She will make antibodies to fight against the exact germ her body has just detected. Every teaspoon of breastmilk contains about 3 million germ fighting cells.

There are thousands of different ingredients in breastmilk. Scientists don't even understand them all and how they all work. New things are being discovered every day. Some of them are food for your body to give you energy and help you grow and help your brain develop. Some of them help you to feel less stressed or reduce pain. Human milk adapts according to the environment the mother and baby are in and changes every single day. The water content may change when it gets hotter to meet the baby's needs. The fat content will change. Many of the thousands of separate ingredients in human milk make life hard for the bad viruses and bacteria that cause diseases and make us ill.

Human milk has lots of superstar ingredients that help protect us from disease. It contains a protein called alpha-lactalbumin that can destroy cancer cells. Research scientists are studying breast milk to help them create medicine that might help people with cancer.

Human milk contains macrophages (which means 'big eater' in Greek). These are white blood cells that go around looking for bad bacteria and things that might cause disease and eat them.

If you are worried I'm starting to bang on about a thousand ingredients and this could take a while, I promise I'm not going to talk about gangliosides, arachidonic acid, stem cells, thiamine, plasmalogens, IgE, SIgA, IgD, FIL, leptin, erythropoietin or phenylalanine or lysophosphatidylethanolamine or cytidine diphosphate choline. If I started to try and talk about all the different ingredients in human milk it would fill a book 100 times longer than this one!

Here are just three more:

1. **Epidermal growth factor**: helps a baby's digestive system to develop. Doctors who look after premature babies in hospital know that tiny babies who get human milk are better protected from a dangerous disease called NEC (necrotising enterocolitis), which can damage their intestines.

2. **Lysozyme**: attacks bad bacteria by messing around with their cell walls.

3. **Lactoferrin**: helps babies absorb iron and also stops nasty bacteria using iron to survive, which reduces the baby's risk of getting diseases. It helps protect the baby against dangerous bacteria like *staphylococci* and *E. coli*.

Bacteria have a bad reputation. It's a word that we think of when we think of germs and dirtiness, but not all bacteria are bad. If I said we want babies to be covered in bacteria, you'd probably think BLEURGH. But bacteria can also be great!

Friendly bacteria do all sorts of important jobs. Without friendly bacteria, we'd be in big trouble. The whole planet would be covered in millions of years' worth of dead animals and old leaves for starters. Without bacteria, we wouldn't be able to make cheese or yoghurt. Bacteria keep soil healthy and help plants to grow. The bacteria inside our bodies are important too and we have a lot of them. We might have two kilograms worth of bacteria in our bodies when we are an adult. That weighs as much as two big water bottles. And when you consider that bacteria are so tiny they are smaller than a full stop, that's a LOT of bacteria. Friendly bacteria keep our insides healthy by helping us to digest food. Scientists even think that our good bacteria might help people to deal with stress, help us to sleep and help us to be a healthy weight!

Of course, there are nasty bacteria around too. That's why grown-ups talk endlessly about you needing to wash your hands. They can upset our tummies and give us nasty coughs and ear infections. Some not-so-friendly bacteria can even mean babies get seriously ill and need to go to hospital. However, if the friendly bacteria have moved into a baby's tummy first, the bad guys don't have as much space to make their homes. A mother's milk contains special sugars called oligosaccharides. These aren't sugars that give us energy like the sugars you now eat in fruit or biscuits. At first, when they found them, scientists were confused. Why are there special sugars in breastmilk that babies can't even digest? Then they realised that these sugars aren't to feed the *babies*! They are there to feed the millions of *good bacteria* that live inside us. That's how important the bacteria are. Those oligosaccharide sugars keep the good guys happy and healthy so the bad guys are kept under control.

When you are first born, your mum holds you against her and her skin touches your skin. We want all parents to have that special skin-to-skin cuddle with their babies. Not just because cuddles feel lovely and help to keep us warm, but also so you can meet all those friendly bacteria. You're not just saying hello to your mum for the first time. You're meeting the whole family and there are millions of them. Your mum has a unique family of friendly bacteria and she got lots of them from *her* mum. They live on skin as well as in your tummy. Your mum gives birth to you and you pick up the first lot of friends on your way out (yes, I am talking about your mother's vagina). Then, when you are held skin-to-skin, you get a bunch more.

Babies come out looking a bit sticky. They might have white waxy stuff on them called vernix and they don't look sparkly clean like the babies on adverts. All that sticky stuff is great for picking up friendly bacteria and keeping the bad guys away. The bacteria that your parents have as their friendly bacteria are not the same as your neighbours and your school friends. We all have a unique set of friends – a bit like a fingerprint.

After a bit of hanging out skin-to-skin, you wriggle up to mum's breast and have a first few sips of milk. She might help you to get there. Your tummy and your gut are then meeting all of the millions of new friends they need too. Babies' tummies are very small – about the size of a cherry – so one teaspoon of colostrum at the very start is all that's needed.

Breasts are only a bit about milk. When a baby comes to the breast, it might not simply be because they are hungry. They aren't just there to do some drinking. Sucking and being close is important too. Dummies were invented for babies to suck on because sometimes mums aren't around and babies often feel calmer when they suck. When breasts are there, breasts do lots of different jobs. They keep babies warm. They keep them calm. They help their brains to develop and help them to feel safe and secure in a new scary world. In Germany, they don't say a baby is 'breastfeeding'. They call it 'stillen'. That means being calmed, relaxed, made peaceful. No mention of milk at all. In America, they say a mother is 'nursing' her baby. Now that might partly be because they want to avoid saying the word 'breast', but it's also because when you 'nurse' someone, you are caring for them and looking after them.

It might be that your mum didn't breastfeed you. Some mums don't feel that breastfeeding is right for them for lots of different reasons. They can still do all the cuddles, and cuddling skin-on-skin gives you a chance to meet some of those friendly bacteria. Some mums really want to breastfeed, but find it difficult and don't get the help they need. They might stop before they want to. Even if a baby gets just a little bit of breastmilk, they are receiving that special medicine and millions and millions of vital cells.

When the time comes for you to think about breastfeeding, the world is likely to be a very different place. You might be sending text messages to your best friend with just your mind while instructing your robot chef to make your dinner with food delivered by a drone. Or maybe not. Whatever happens, your body is getting ready right now for you to breastfeed. We'll talk more about being a mum in another chapter.

A day in the life of a baby

Elsie is 10 weeks old. Here's her day.

6.30am Woke up (except that makes it sound like I actually had a night's sleep. I was awake at 1am, 4am and 5.15am if you must know). I sleep right next to milky parent (who has useful nipples).

6.35am Nappy change. My poo is bright yellow and very soft. It smells like biscuits. My friendly bacteria keep my poo smelling rather nice when I'm just having milk.

6.45am Milk. Both breasts. Back to the first again. I was sick a bit afterwards. Cuddly parent (no working nipples but still good at cuddles) had to change my clothes. It was worth it.

7.15am Nap in milky parent's arms.

7.45am Nap in cuddly parent's arms.

8am Bit more breast time.

8.30am Kick around on my mat. Nappy emergency!

8.45am Take big brother to school. Nap in pram. Someone pats me on the head. Saw a dog.

9.10am Shops. Another dog.

9.45am Breast please! I have a trapped air bubble and it really hurts. Phew! Milky parent helped me get it out.

10am–11am Sleep.

11am Cuddle. Milky parent drops a bit of toast on my head. Nappy!

11.30am Breast please!

1pm Walk to health visitor clinic. Milky parent carries me in a sling and I have a little sleep. I get weighed and everyone is happy because that means I'm growing properly and getting enough milk. Milky parent asks someone if I should be given some water to drink when it's hot. She's told I shouldn't have any water and breastmilk has loads of water in it anyway. Someone records my weight in a red book. Saw lots of babies. No dogs. Nappy!

1.45pm Really hungry on way home and cry a lot.

2pm Breast please! Breast and a cuddle and a sleep. Nappy!

3pm Pick up big brother from school.

3.45pm Play with big brother. He reads me a story. I watch him eat a banana. They look very interesting but I won't get any food until I'm 6 months old. I only need milk for now.

4pm Breast please! Nappy! Sleep.

5pm Watch milky parent make dinner. Cuddly parent comes home. I get a bath and a cuddle.

6pm I cry a lot. I'm not quite sure why. I just cry a lot at this time. Do I always need a reason? I don't want to go to sleep. I don't want to be put in my chair. I'm sort of hungry but I'm also sort of tired. I DON'T KNOW (but cuddles help!).

6pm–9.30pm Lots of breast please. Nappy!

10pm Fall asleep after cuddly parent walks me around singing a song but awake again at 11.45pm and 4.30am for breast please!

Here's what some mums say is the best thing about breastfeeding:

It solves almost every problem: hunger, thirst, fear, loneliness, boredom. No need to flap about and panic trying all kinds of different things, just settle in for a cuddle with baby.

For me, the bond is like nothing else. I love cuddling and feeding and being close.

Knowing that my babies and I will be less likely to develop certain illnesses because I was able to breastfeed them.

The feelings of love and bonding, and how happy it makes the baby.

I love how I grew my baby inside and out. Looking at them and thinking, 'Yeah, my milk did that!'

It's free! (Honestly this was a big motivator for me with twins as it would have been well over £1,000 in formula for the first year. In the end I only bought one 'just in case' tin and only used half of it).

It gives my baby everything he needs without me having to think about it. If he cries I just breastfeed him – it solves everything!

The connection you feel. There's no way to describe it. It's the best feeling, surpassing happiness and love because it's both of those and more combined.

It's so convenient – no remembering to buy formula, sterilising bottles, going downstairs in the middle of the night to make up a bottle, don't have to take lots of stuff out with you. On a deeper level, it creates an amazing bond between you and your baby – something special only you can have with them.

Not having to carry loads of stuff with me everywhere I go. It's me, my baby and my boobs. Job done!

Breastfeeding helped me survive becoming a parent!

Lots of extra lovely cuddles and that when it's cold at night time I don't have to get out of bed to make a bottle!

The recipe changes every feed, giving baby exactly what they need at that moment. More water when they're hot and thirsty, sleepy hormones at bed time, medicine when they're poorly. And it comes with snuggles.

*NO WASHING UP! *high fives all around**

It's the way nature intended us to feed our babies.

Photography by © RÅN studio

My milk has super powers/antibodies that fight nasties for the baby which protects it like a shield as it grows up.

Best type of cuddle imaginable.

It makes me feel calm and happy, and my baby (well, toddler) thinks it's better than ice cream.

I'm too lazy to be getting up in the middle of the night and leaving my warm cosy bed to be faffing about making bottles. Plus, the snuggles constantly are incredible.

It's cuddly. Best thing I ever did.

I love that it's the best drink in the world, and it's made specifically for her. How special can anyone be to have a drink made for them!

It doesn't cost a penny yet it's the best ever start for a baby in their life – liquid gold.

I make milk without even doing anything. It just, happens! Sometimes I just stand in a room and milk starts to flow and it's like a super power.

In this busy life, it gives me multiple opportunities to stop, reset and enjoy cuddles. Eleven years can go by pretty quickly and tiny toes don't stay tiny for very long. It gives me a moment to appreciate the little things.

Photography by © RÅN studio

CHAPTER TWO

Here come the buds

You've changed a lot in the last few years. You learnt to walk. You learnt to use a toilet. You learnt to eat spaghetti. You learnt to read and write. You learnt how to be a good friend. Now you and your friends are about to go through a new stage in life. Your body is getting ready to become an adult who might one day have a baby, but it takes a long time.

The story of your breasts started when you were a nubbin of a baby inside your mother's womb. When you were just a few weeks old, and about the size of a sesame seed, your chest area started to get thicker and what we call 'the milk line' started to develop. It's also called the 'mammary ridge' (there's that mammal word again). You got one on each side of your body. The lines became hollow over time and they formed milk ducts, which are the tubes the milk flows down when you have your own baby one day.

When you are born, you have the nipples and the beginning of milk ducts and that's it. But even then, it's amazing what they can do. Do you know some babies are born being able to drip tiny amounts of milk from their own little mini-breasts? It's sometimes called 'witch's milk' because there were once old tales of how witches fed on the drips of milk. That's probably not a story you want to tell someone who's just had a new baby and you're meant to be saying their baby is cute. It happens because when the baby is born it has some of mum's hormones in its system and the mini-breasts get a bit confused. It doesn't last long.

Then your breasts don't do much for a long time. For many years, nothing changes. That's all the time you're eating spaghetti and learning how to use the toilet and learning to read and making new friends.

Sometime between being eight years old and 13, they start to wake up again. It can be slightly earlier and slightly later for some people – everyone is different.

Do you remember that hormones are those chemicals your body makes to send messages and switch things on? Your brain makes hormones in places called the HYPOTHALAMUS and the PITUITARY GLAND. Don't worry if you can't pronounce those words – lots of adults can't. The brain hormones have even better names like 'gonadotropin-releasing hormone' and 'follicle-stimulating hormone'.

Most adults don't know about those either, which might be useful. You can say things like, 'I'm so sorry I can't tidy my room. I need to rest because my hypothalamus is producing gonadotropin-releasing hormone and telling my pituitary gland to make follicle-stimulating hormone and the luteinizing hormone, and I need to have a lie-down'. Or maybe write it in a note if you can't say it.

The brain hormones then send messages to your ovaries. They are the useful organs either side of your womb that make the teeny-weeny eggs that might be half a baby one day. In pictures, it looks like your womb has groovy deer antlers.

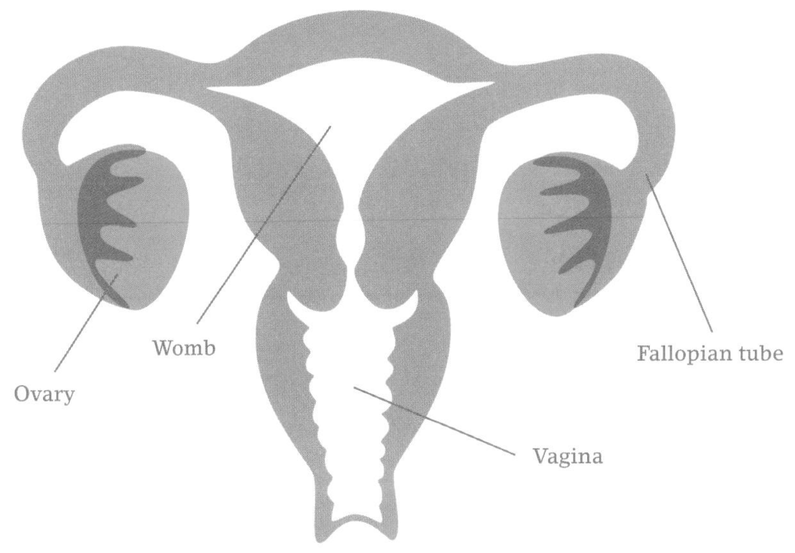

The ovaries get the hormone message from your brain and think, 'OK, time to start making breasts' and they produce a hormone called OESTROGEN (Americans call it estrogen: I don't know why they want to save on Os).

Oestrogen is your breasts' friend. I could say your breasts' best friend, but that would make the progesterone hormone feel sad because progesterone is important too.

Oestrogen tells the body to start changing things around your chest and to start collecting fat there. Progesterone and oestrogen start developing the important bits that will form your working breast. At the end of it all, you will have breasts filled with milk ducts and lobes and alveoli (that look sort of like clusters of grapes). It will look like a bushy tree with some of the milk ducts being thick bigger branches and some being like twigs. At the end of the twigs are the lobules and the tiny alveoli where the milk is made.

But you don't start with all that. The first thing you might notice is a slightly tender nipple. You may feel something before you can see anything. One nipple or both might feel sore or tingly. A bump will start to develop behind the nipple – about the size of a pea or a little bit bigger.

This isn't going to happen in half an hour while you are watching TV, or even overnight, but slowly and gradually. The whole process of going from a tingly nipple to breasts that look like grown-up breasts takes several years.

If your bumps start to come when you are younger, it won't mean you'll end up with bigger breasts and if they start to come when you are older, it won't mean you'll end up with smaller ones.

The bumps behind the nipple get a little bigger and they're called buds. You've got fat collecting there while the milk-making tree is very slowly starting to grow at the same time. It's normal to feel an itch or an ache, but just because that's normal, it doesn't mean you shouldn't talk to someone if you are worried.

A LOT of people notice that one bud is growing before the other one. That's a normal part of mammogenesis (science word for breast development). Try, 'I'm sorry I can't do the washing up right now, I'm in the middle of mammogenesis'.

The bump gets a bit bigger and your nipple might start to change and get darker and stick out more. The coloured circle around the nipple is called the areola (pronounced 'ah ree oh la' or sometimes 'uh REE oh la' or 'AH REE oh la'). The areola often has little bumps on it that look a bit like pimples. This doesn't mean your teenage spots are starting on your breast. They are special glands called Montgomery's glands. They make your nipples their very own moisturiser. Some people notice these bumps sticking up and some people don't.

The main part of the breast eventually gets bigger and fattier. The areola and nipple might stick out by themselves

Breasts can be round, tear-drop shaped, a bit pointy or fairly flat. It's common for breasts or nipples to not be exactly the same on both sides.

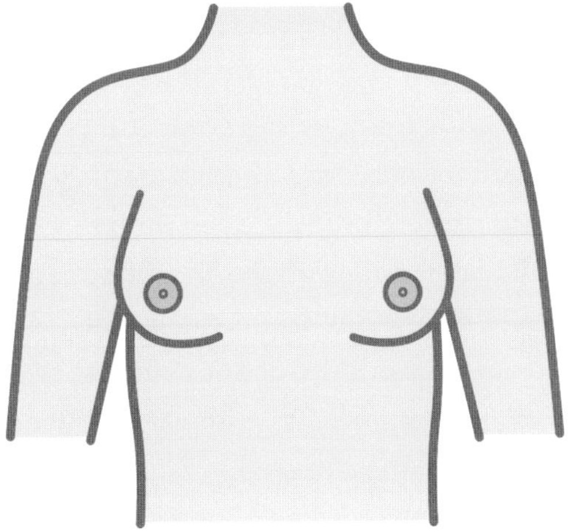

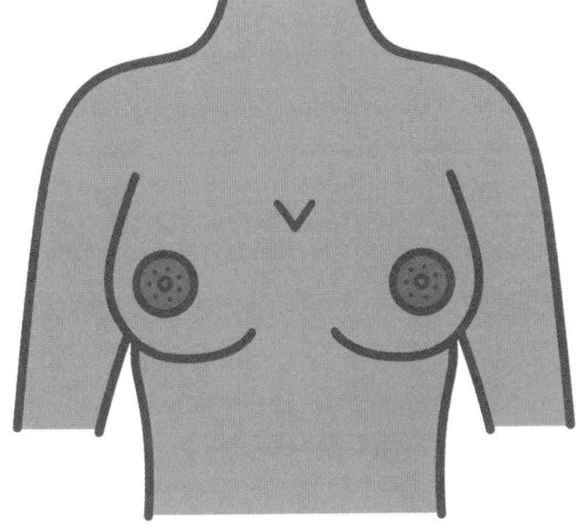

Around the areola, we often have little bumps called Montgomery's glands. Sometimes they stick out but not always.

and make a second mound, but eventually the areola bump settles down until the nipple is the only bit that sticks out more for most people (but not everyone).

You've probably noticed how I keep saying, 'Some people get this, but not everyone' and, 'Most people get this, but not everyone'. There are so many ways to be normal. That's true for everything in life and it's also true about the way breasts develop.

About a year and a half to three years after your breasts start to develop, your period comes along. This isn't a book about periods, but I need to mention them as they are connected to breasts. Even though you are not going to have children for a long time (if you want to), your body is getting ready for the day when you might.

As well as helping your breasts to grow, your oestrogen and progesterone hormones have been helping your ovaries and womb too. The inside of your womb is making itself comfy just in case a tiny baby ever needs to grow there. It's making itself thick and cosy by building up layers of blood and body tissue. And once a month, one of your ovaries releases an egg to practise for the day when it might meet a sperm (the male seed it needs to join with to start making a new person). If the egg doesn't get used, it just passes into the toilet or your underwear and it's very tiny, so it won't even be noticed. The egg passes through your womb and out of your vagina and it's like the womb thinks, 'OK, no baby this month'. All the comfy layers made from blood aren't needed, and they start to get cleaned out ready to start thickening again for the next month's egg in a couple of weeks.

When the egg has gone, very slowly the layers on the inside of the womb come away and start to trickle out of your body through your vagina. You can catch the blood using things like sticky towels – sanitary towels – that stick onto your pants. But some people use other things too. You can buy special underwear that soaks up blood. Some women use squishy cups that go inside the vagina, or a tampon, which is made from paper and cotton wool and string and also goes inside your vagina, to collect or absorb the blood rather than waiting for it to come out.

When your periods first begin, it might not happen every month. You might have gaps. Then it will come roughly every month, though it can vary from around every 28 days to every 35. In the end, you settle down into a predictable pattern you get used to.

When you first start your periods, the blood is a tiny amount. You've got lots of time to get yourself sorted and find something to catch it. It's not like you are sitting there in a red puddle all of a sudden. Sometimes your first period might even look brown rather than red, and that's completely normal. Gradually the amount gets bigger, but even women who have been having periods for years pass a few teaspoons of blood a day rather than the red puddle thing. As time goes by, women get a feeling when it's happening. They might notice their body starts to feel different, and they may also have a clue when it's going to happen because it's been a certain number of days or weeks since the last time. Women often know the exact day when the blood might start to arrive.

During each period, your breasts change too. The alveoli at the ends of the milk ducts, which will make the milk, develop slightly more each month. As each month goes by, the oestrogen and progesterone take it in turns to grow milk ducts and alveoli. Some women feel tenderness in their breast at certain times of the month as the hormones change the way the breasts store water and they can feel fuller. They don't get bigger for ever and ever. Eventually your grown-up breasts decide they are done for now and you stay about the same size until you might get pregnant one day.

While your breasts are changing, there are other changes too. You develop hair under your arms and between your legs near your vulva and vagina. Usually pubic hair (the hair between your legs) starts to arrive about six months after your breasts first start to change.

You'll probably have lots of questions, and I've answered some of them below:

Do breasts hurt when they grow?
They can a little. More of an ache than lots of pain. They can feel itchy and tingly too. It might not feel comfortable sleeping on your front or it might hurt when someone bangs into you.

You said it can be normal for one nipple to change before the other and for things to look lop-sided. Really?
Yes, really. Here's something not everyone knows – loads and loads of women have breasts that are slightly different sizes. LOADS. You may not know it by looking at them with their clothes on, but it's super normal to have nipples or breasts that look different.

That's even more true when your breasts are first starting out. It might be a year before they start evening up. Remember, no one is going to look at them as closely as you are. For a start, you are looking at them from above, which makes the angle different, but even in a mirror you are studying them when you are standing still. Other people see them under clothes when you are moving around and busy doing things. If you are very worried they are different sizes, you can use a bra later to sort things out. We'll talk about that a bit more in the chapter on bras.

My nipples don't stick out.
Nipples can be flat. They can stick out and they can even cave in slightly. We call that being inverted. Most people have

them slightly inverted when they are younger, and when mammogenesis begins, their nipples start to stick out a bit more. But not everyone. Some women have nipples that only stick out when they are cold or if their nipples get rubbed or when a baby is feeding. Nipples can point up or down. There are lots of different types of normal. Have I mentioned that already?

I've got a hair on my nipple.

Yes. You may have a few. They are usually quite small hairs. Hair can grow all over our body including on our nipples. I would just let it do its thing. Pulling it out can be painful and cause problems. It really is normal.

I've got thin red lines on my breasts.

Assuming you haven't been scratched by a grumpy cat and you otherwise feel OK, these sound like stretchmarks. Sometimes our breasts grow quickly, and the skin doesn't stretch fast enough. It can happen to pregnant women's tummies sometimes as well. Stretch marks start out looking red and noticeable, but they fade as time goes on, so you won't have red lines forever.

My breasts feel lumpy.

When your breasts first start to develop, they will start with the lump that feels like a big pea behind your nipple. Later, when your milk-making alveoli and lobes start to arrive, they can feel a bit lumpy too. You may also find your breasts can feel a bit lumpy at certain times of the month when you are having your periods. When you get older, it's recommended to check your breasts each month to make sure all the lumps are the ones you recognise, and everything is normal for you. Most new lumps are nothing to worry about, but your doctor can check and help you if you are worried.

My breasts haven't started to change.
Is there anything I can do to speed things up?
I'm afraid there is nothing you can do. There is all sorts of nonsense out there about exercises you can do or even special creams you can use, but there really isn't anything that can change how and when your hormones wake up and start to send messages. Your body will do its own thing in its own time. Usually we experience puberty at roughly the same time as our mothers and older sisters did, so perhaps you can ask them what their experiences were. If zero has happened by the time you are 14 – no bud, nothing – it's usually recommended to have a chat with your GP (family doctor), who is there to help you.

I have a bulge in my armpit that feels a bit sore.
Breasts go up further into your armpit than you might realise. They are like the shape of a drip and the thin bit – called the tail of Spence – goes right under your arm. Some people have an extra bulge as they have even more breast tissue up there. It might even feel achy at times. If you are a mum making milk one day, you might feel a fullness in your armpit which is quite far away from where the drinking is happening!

Do you know some people even have an extra nipple? When you were a baby, do you remember you had a milk ridge – the line which goes down your body? For some people, extra bits of the line hang around when the rest has gone. Some people have an extra nipple, often under their breasts and above their tummy button. They look a bit like a mole (not the animal that digs tunnels, the coloured freckles we have on our skin) and they are usually much smaller than the other nipples. They are nothing to worry about, and might be handy if you ever have triplets (although without a breast, the third baby might get a bit cross at the lack of milk). About 1 in 18 people have an extra nipple, so chances are someone in your class at school has one. I wouldn't recommend going around asking everyone though.

Can boys get breasts?

Some boys do get a fuller chest as they become a teenager. That might be because there are some fat deposits on their chest. Some boys get a tingly nipple or even a bump like girls too. It doesn't last long and usually goes away in a year or so. It's not that unusual, but boys can worry that they aren't normal if it happens and may feel uncomfortable going without wearing a top. If it happens to your brother or your friend, you can reassure them that it happens to a lot of people as the hormones are getting themselves sorted out. I wouldn't bring it up unless they do.

I don't know if I need a bra.

You can start wearing a bra when it feels right for you. There are lots of options. There are soft vest tops. There are bras designed for smaller, newer breasts. Some women – even when they are adults – don't feel they need to wear a bra. Bras can be useful if your breasts feel heavier or if you want to do a lot of running and exercise and you want your breasts to have more support. Some people wear bras as they feel more comfortable and confident having an extra layer under thinner clothing. Some people might tell you that you need to get one, but don't do it just because they say so. What feels right for you is probably right. You might buy one, but not necessarily wear it every day. See how you go. We'll talk more about bras later.

Some people talk about having surgery on their breasts. What's that all about?

Have you heard of plastic surgery? It's sometimes called cosmetic surgery. Some people have operations to change the shape of their nose. Or they want to change how their lips look. A small number of grown-ups do have surgery on their breasts to make them look different – bigger or smaller. A surgeon can make breasts bigger by sewing a bag of silicone gel or sometimes salty water under your skin. No one is allowed to have the operation until they are at least 18 and even then it's a big decision that has to be thought

about very, very carefully, as it might make it harder for someone to feed a baby if they end up being a mother. It can sometimes have other complications and it can take a long time to recover and be painful. The bags don't last forever, and women will need another operation to replace them after a few years. Some women feel it's something they want to risk doing because after their breasts have finished growing, they want them to look different and they think the surgery will help them feel happier. What would you say to a friend who said they wanted to have plastic surgery?

"Some people might tell you that you need to get one, but don't do it just because they say so. What feels right for you is probably right."

Tessa, 21

I was about Year 5 or Year 6 in school and I hadn't developed really at all at that point but my friend had a bra. It must have been about size AAAA! She didn't really need one but it was so exciting that we were growing up. We were both in the toilet and she suggested I tried it on. It was a coming of age thing. I was growing into an actual lady. It felt like a really big thing. My friend let me keep it on and borrow her bra and I came home wearing it. I remember my mum was horrified! She said I didn't need a bra. I was upset to be reminded I wasn't grown up yet. I did listen to my mum though. I didn't really need one. I didn't wear one again for ages. I was probably about Year 8 when I started to develop. At that point, it started to be embarrassing if you didn't wear one in school. In the PE room, people started to make fun of you. Just a bit. I had one friend who didn't want to wear a bra and people used to sometimes say things.

Now I'm 21, I've just finished doing a fine arts degree. In art school, it's accepted that you can be what you want to

"I was probably about Year 8 when I started to develop. At that point, it started to be embarrassing if you didn't wear one in school. In the PE room, people started to make fun of you. Just a bit."

be and wear what you want to wear. You don't have to wear a bra if you don't want to. People are walking around naked doing performance art – not all the time! People might wear pyjamas if they want to. For the past three years, I've been moulded to thinking that what you look like and what you wear is not the most important thing. But in everyday life, away from art school, there is an expectation that you would wear a bra if you were going out. You might be judged if you didn't.

I think there is a pressure on some girls to look a certain way. Instagram and Facebook seem to have pictures of women in bikinis and there's a lot of focus on body shape. There's pressure to be toned and tanned and look a certain way and boobs come into that. Younger people at secondary school seem to be more aware of what they look like than I was at their age. There's pressure to look a certain way and post on social media looking a certain way.

I remember when I was younger we talked about periods at school. That was really frightening! But there was nothing about boobs. We never talked about boobs in school, in sex education. My mum would answer my questions and explain how I was growing and I could talk to my friends as well. I always had a good group of friends. But we never talked about breasts changing at school.

CHAPTER THREE

Bras

Have you ever been in a department store and walked through the bra department? It's a forest of lace and frilly things and straps and clips and AA and D cups and teeny-weeny hangers. There are so many different types of bras in different shapes and colours and sizes. And people don't even see them most of the time. They are usually hidden under clothes. You can buy a bra that costs £150 and it's not even made of diamonds – just lace and metal and cotton. It's normal for a bra to cost £20–£40. A lot of women spend more money on their bra than they do on their outside clothes.

Let's think about the world of bras. What are they for? Does everyone wear them? What different types are there? How do you know which is the right size for you?

For a long time, humans didn't wear bras. Throughout recorded history, cultures have bobbed back and forth about how they wanted breasts to look. Sometimes breasts were highlighted and pushed up and made more obvious. Sometimes breasts were pushed down and flattened and hidden away. Sometimes a piece of fabric went under breasts or around them or a piece of jewellery did.

If you read a history of things women wore under their clothes I GUARANTEE you'll end up feeling angry. Women

often wore things that were uncomfortable or even painful. They sometimes couldn't even breathe properly. In Victorian times, women carried around a little bottle of 'smelling salts' that they might sniff if they were starting to feel faint because the chemicals in the bottle would shock them into coming round. That's how normal it was for women to feel faint and their clothing was usually to blame.

Women couldn't run properly, although that might have been considered unladylike for other reasons too. ('Unladylike' – *bleurgh* – there's a word to hate.) They couldn't ride bicycles because their clothes were too restrictive and when they started trying, they often got really badly hurt because their clothes got in the way. Women who wanted to ride bicycles tried to change their clothing – they asked for 'emancipation' clothes. Emancipation means getting greater freedom and being liberated. It's not a coincidence that the more women have felt free and in control of their own lives, the more their clothing has become more comfortable and flexible.

Women throughout history often wore corsets that squeezed their body. Sometimes they were made of metal. Imagine right now wearing metal bars across your body to squish you into shape because society tells you that's what you are supposed to do. And if you tried to take them off, people would judge you and say you were being shocking and rude.

And later on, when it wasn't metal, women wore corsets made from whalebone. I doubt the whales were too thrilled about that either. Corsets meant you couldn't relax and not only were you kept upright, but you were also squeezed with laces at the back.

Gradually corsets started to change. Women wanted to be able to do different things that required moving and doctors realised that women were suffering from a range of health conditions. How do you think you digest food when your tummy is squished to the smallest shape possible?

As women became freer in society and had more power, corsets became smaller and then mostly disappeared. Anyone who wears a corset today (and sometimes it still happens) is doing it for fun and they should be in charge of when they want to put it on and take it off!

In the 20th century bras that we might recognise came along. And as different materials were invented, bras were made of newer fabrics that might be stretchier or more comfortable.

This doesn't mean that the power thing has been completely sorted out. Sometimes women are under pressure for their breasts to be a particular shape, even in the modern era. In the 1950s, bras were very pointy. Today, women are often given messages about how nipples are not supposed to stick out through their clothing, and some women wear bras just for this reason. Elbows fine. Nipples not. You can show your ear but not the shape of your nipple under layers of clothing. Who makes these rules? Shops now sell bras that are made of a thicker foam material and they even say on the packaging 'smooth' and 'discreet' and 'invisible'. You can even buy flower-shaped things that you stick over your nipples to really make sure they can't be seen!

Have you ever known anyone to suffer physically or emotionally because they saw the shape of someone's bra through some clothing or the shape of a nipple? Because I haven't. Perhaps, instead of women buying moulded 'smooth'

“The idea that breasts should be round and high on your body is a lie. Plenty of people have breasts that droop and hang down.”

'invisible' bras (which cost a lot of money) we should buy anyone worried about seeing the shape of a bra a blindfold to wear when they go out. If anyone says to you, 'I can see the shape of your bra through your clothes', you can reply, 'I'd be worried if you couldn't. It might suggest you have issues with your vision'. And if someone says, 'I can see your nipples', you can say, 'This is where most women keep them'.

If you visit the bra department, you might get the impression that women's breasts are all roughly the same shape. They all appear to be round in the same way. They are symmetrical. A lot of new bras have a cup made of material that sticks out all by itself and your real breasts hide inside.

The idea that breasts should be round and high on your body is a lie. Plenty of people have breasts that droop and hang down. One 23-year-old called Chidera Eggerue started the hashtag #saggyboobsmatter and she posts on social media talking about how her droopier breasts are normal and worth celebrating. She was bored of trying to buy bras and the women on the packaging not looking like her. She encourages women to love their natural selves and be 'body positive' and not think breasts have to look a certain way. Your breasts might hang more loosely or be lower than breasts you see in pictures.

Chidera Eggerue was interviewed by *The Guardian* newspaper:

'I discovered from about 15 that I had saggy boobs, and remember going to the high street and feeling frustrated that none of the bras would fit… At the time, it was only small-boobed women who were 'allowed' to not wear a bra – because there wasn't much to judge,' she says. As a 'larger-boobed woman', her decision attracted a lot of unwanted attention. 'People would say: "You're jiggling too much. I can see your nipples. This is bad. Cover yourself up." I couldn't understand why. Every time I asked somebody, the answer was: "Because you're a girl. Because you're a woman." I knew that wasn't really an acceptable answer. I had to challenge it…'

'Ultimately, nobody has the right to tell you how to love your body, which is more than just a collection of cells and functions. It is home to a remarkable, intelligent young woman. It is a witness to all the wonderful things you have ever encountered. How you look is the least important thing; never underestimate the importance of your presence…'

'When people stare, it can leave you feeling vulnerable or scared. But I can assure you that those who look do so out of curiosity rather than disgust. You cannot control how others view you and it's important to remember that those who are the most critical of others tend to be insecure in themselves.'

'When it comes to your friends, anyone who makes you doubt yourself is someone you should try to spend less time with. Friends should encourage you to be yourself more, not less.'

If you do want to wear a bra and find one that fits, they aren't always completely comfortable even today. There are still bits of metal and hard plastic sometimes. They can feel tight and they can rub and feel itchy.

Why do women bother spending money on something that isn't always that comfortable anyway? Some women do like the feeling that their breasts are supported. It can make it easier to run and move if your breasts aren't completely hanging free, especially if a woman has larger breasts. Some women also like how they look. They like the lace and the colour and the frilly bits. Everyone is different and some women have reasons for preferring to wear a bra.

Liz, 38

You may hear that bras are not necessary. That it's better for breast health not to wear them, and certainly, if you are comfortable ditching the itch and confinement of bras, go right ahead. You may also hear from the body positivity community (of which I'm a MASSIVE fan and wholly recommend everyone getting stuck into) and from various corners of feminism and the Women's Rights movement that burning your bra is Liberating and Symbolic and Important. Again, whatever floats your boat. If you want to make a political statement about everybody being celebrated, not just the perkiest, and feel that #saggyboobsmatter, please, please follow your heart.

But I want to make an important point – bras are not needless to many – you need to follow your comfort too. I cannot abide being boobsplained to by someone with smaller breasts than me, that I would be better off without a bra – walk a mile with my baps and you'll be screaming for one! (Some) large breasts need a bra. Boobs with dense breast tissue can really hurt without a bra. My balance is off without a bra. The weight of my boobs hurts without a bra. Bras lift the breasts so that the skin underneath can breathe. Clothes are not cut to fit and flatter breasts around belly button level!!

If it's comfortable for you to swing free, I'm all for it. I detest the idea that we should cover the jiggle and hide the nips, but I also don't get on with the idea that we should feel bras are unnecessary. You do you and let others worry about themselves. Self-care is important, and if that means wearing a bra, embrace and own that.

When do you buy your first bra? When you want to. And by the way, there are some women who are 40 years old who still haven't bought their first bra.

Do you want to get one because all your friends are getting one? You can buy one because of that if you want to. We're not going to pretend wanting to be like your friends doesn't matter. Everyone – even grown-ups – can feel a pressure to fit in with the people around them.

What about if someone in your family is saying you NEED one? Ask them why they think that. Are they making a good case? On the other hand, you might want one and your family might not think it's right. Explain why it's important to you or write them a note. It should be your decision. Or you could leave this book open and highlight this paragraph and I'll do the job for you. HEY, YOU! THE OWNER OF THIS BOOK WOULD LIKE TO TALK ABOUT BUYING A BRA! THANK YOU. Flick to the end of this chapter and you'll find some letters you can highlight and leave lying around.

Bras come in lots of different sizes. A measurement is taken around your ribcage where the lower part of the bra will sit. That's usually in inches in the UK, but sometimes in centimetres. Then there is a cup size – the cup is the fabric that goes around your breast. If your breasts stick out a lot from your body, you will need a bigger cup size. If your nipples are closer to your ribs, you'll have a smaller cup size. So, someone who has a small back and ribcage and breasts that don't take up much space might wear a 28A bra. (AA is a really small cup size, E is a bigger one). Somebody with a small ribcage and back but breasts that stick out further might still be 28 on the inches but a D cup.

You can get cup sizes that go up to K or L but it can be harder to buy them in most shops. You will know women that wear 34C or 36DD (they sometimes have double letter sizes too, so 36DD is in between 36D and 36E). One woman, throughout her life, may have worn 28A, 30B, 32C, 34C, 34B and 36B. What!? How come one woman might wear so many different sizes? At the beginning, she was growing and her breasts were developing. Then maybe her body changed shape a bit, because it's really normal for women to sometimes be heavier at certain times in their life. Then maybe she got pregnant and had a baby and her breasts changed shape. One of those bras might have been a special breastfeeding bra with clips that help you to open up the cups so your baby can feed. Some women might have breasts that are very different sizes and they might put extra padding in one side of their bra, so they look more symmetrical when they have clothes on. Some bras are made from nothing but fabric. Some have plastic bits to give a shape. Some have 'underwiring' – semi-circles of wire that go under your breast. Bras often have straps that go on your shoulders, but not always. Sometimes the straps are in different places to fit under different types of clothing. You can even get bras with no straps at all!

Shops have bra fitters that can measure you to help you find the right size. A LOT of women wear the wrong size. Often women have a cup size that is too small. So someone might be wearing a 36D when really they should be a 34E. I know someone (OK, it was me) who thought they were a 34DD and it turned out they were a 32G! Wearing the wrong size can cause problems. It can squash breasts in weird ways, but it can also leave you with red lines on your skin or an aching back and shoulders.

Another complication is that different types of bras might fit differently. Women might be one size in one shop and a different size in another. So often you just have to try a bra on and see how it fits. I know this sounds complicated, but finding shoes that fit can be a hassle too and we're used to doing that. The wrong size shoe can hurt. You might wear one size when you buy a sandal but when you buy a pair of boots, you choose a different size. You need to try them on before you buy them. Bra measuring sounds a faff, but you don't have to worry about all that right at the start.

At the beginning, it's much easier. Your first bra (if you want to have one) is usually made of soft material and more of a crop top thing than a wire/hard plastic lace thing.

Sophie, 48

A couple of years ago I stopped wearing a bra. I mostly stopped wearing a bra because it made sense to me that our bodies are quite well designed to support themselves, and that using a contraption like the bra was stopping my muscles and ligaments doing their job well.

Bras haven't been around for that long; they were apparently invented in the late 19th century. How did women manage before them?

After I stopped wearing a bra, I found it absolutely fascinating that it only took a couple of weeks for my breasts to stop hurting when I jumped up or down, or when I ran. I can now run comfortably without wearing one.

So, what are the advantages of not wearing a bra? Better muscle and ligament function around the chest, shoulders and back, and better blood and lymphatic flow (no restrictions from tight fabric), and generally better breast health. It is a lie that not wearing a bra makes breasts sag by the way – research has demonstrated that it is the opposite.

Since I stopped wearing a bra, I've also found myself looking at women in the changing room at my local swimming pool. It feels very odd, not that I'm not wearing one, but that they all are, and aren't questioning it. I'm not saying that nobody should wear one, but that I wish women would ask themselves the question.

It's a very important topic to me because I have a daughter who has just turned nine. Right now, she thinks I'm right, but what will she feel when her breasts start growing, and she wants to do the same thing as her friends?

It's not easy when buying your first bra is seen as a symbol of growing up. Our society lacks the symbols and growing up traditions that other cultures have.

I also understand that there is social pressure and expectations. For instance, a common worry is that your nipples might be showing. I find wearing a vest provides a comfy way to have coverage while still giving freedom. There are also some lovely soft cotton crop top/brassière type items of clothing available.

It's also a symbol of the sexism of our culture: that girls' bodies 'distract' boys. This is ridiculous. Imagine for a second if the reverse to bras was true for boys' genitals (after all, their genitals stick out and dangle while ours don't, so it makes sense). What if boys were told they had to wear a bra to support their willy and testicles and if they didn't it would sag, and 'distract the girls'. Sounds a bit ridiculous, right?

What I'd like to say to my daughter, and to any girl around her age is this: question everything, think for yourself, and most importantly of all, ask yourself: is this right for me?

Let's hear some other women talking about their bra experiences:

Stephanie: I remember my first bra; it was £3, basically two triangles of material for a body that hadn't even yet begun to develop. I was 11 and my dad hit the roof when I came home with it. Nowadays there's no way I would leave the house without one. Like some women have a thing for shoes and handbags, my thing is bras. I have a huge collection of beautiful bras which I'm sad to say no longer fit me due to having a baby and my breast size changing. Also, due to having a baby, I am too poor to replace them all! The best feeling in the world (apart from the flow of oxytocin!) is taking your bra of at the end of the day and getting the 'ahhhh' factor.

Hannah: I remember being embarrassed when I started high school and when changing for PE. All the girls had bras and I was still in crop tops/vests. I was so proud when I finally got my first bra, even though I was such a late developer I had nothing to put in it! I really struggle to get comfy breastfeeding bras so go bra-less at home.

Sam: When I was a child, I wanted big breasts. I remember making a birthday wish for them! It came true. From the end of primary school, I had the biggest breasts in the class and this was great for about three years. Around the middle of secondary school, I started to dislike them a lot. My mum had breast cancer and a mastectomy [an operation to have breasts removed to take the cancer away] at 33. I hoped my breasts would at least last long enough to feed my children, as my mum fed me. Luckily, they have. I hate bras. Even 'proper fitted' aren't comfortable. I think that's part of the package of large breasts? You don't get total comfort ever? You learn to switch off from the discomfort eventually, and plough on with the least uncomfortable bra you find. Since having babies my relationship with clothes, and bras, firmly prioritises comfort. I wear crop top bras. They give just enough support and just enough firmness to stop my breasts swinging and my nipples from being so obvious. I would quite happily exist bra-less if society didn't deem it quite so vulgar.

Nicola: I couldn't wait to get my first bra! I wanted to be a big girl. I now wish I hadn't bothered and I won't be encouraging my daughter to wear one quickly. I love how a good bra makes my boobs look, but I wish I didn't have to wear one. I much prefer to wear one with no underwire these days, but there aren't many in a 36G that have sufficient support. If I'm going out though, underwire is a must! I wish there were more affordable and pretty bras in my size!

Jenni: I don't remember my first bra, but I remember going to buy my first bra with my mum and not having enough breast tissue to fill the smallest size bra so we left with little frilly cotton crop tops.

Kaya: Bras are the bane of my life! I'm 31 and I don't want to wear granny nursing bras, nor do I want to spend £19939292929293 for a pretty bra because I'm a J cup when I'm breastfeeding.

Maddie: Life is more comfortable since I ditched bras for stretchy vest tops. Less back, shoulder and neck pain, no underwire disasters and perkier boobs. I kid you not! Bra fabric is so thick these days. Since when did the nipple become so offensive that we have to hide it under inches of spongy material? Bras made me a feminist. Someone twanged my bra strap when I was 12 and it was my first feminist RAGE.

Sharon: You can get nipple covers for under t-shirts. They stick on the breast. I've seen them in the shops. God forbid a nipple shows through clothing! Why don't men have to wear them? #freethenips

Nikki: No bras for years. They are uncomfy!

Lindsay: Having a properly fitted bra makes all the difference. For years I thought I was 34A then I was properly fitted as a 32E (32F with nursing).

Shelley: I hate having a badly fitting bra and getting that 'double boob' effect on each boob.

Elizabeth: Bras are so frustrating!!! I'm a 36H with one bra size but another shop put me at 36E, so I've been wearing that. The styles I like don't go big enough, they are far too expensive and make my shoulders and back sore. Often they're not available on the high street and if they are, they're ugly! I'm just glad that (having two daughters) I know how to measure them correctly to ensure they don't have the same issues I've had.

Sarah: I love bras: they can make or break an outfit, make running a pleasure, hold your breast pad and stop you leaking everywhere. A well-fitted bra is heaven, a badly fitted one is hell! The best fitters can tell at a glance the shape and size of bra you need. It's an art. I'm a 30E, they're hard to find...

Sharon: Being a larger bust size but quite short; I struggle to find bras that fit well. I hate wired bras because they're so uncomfortable – the wires dig in my armpits and ribs. The straps on most bras slip down and the back rides up. I used to love my breastfeeding bras and I continued to wear them for a lot longer than I needed them for, just because of the comfort.

Beth: I was shamed into wearing bras and I hated them. It seemed overnight my nipples darkened and they could be seen through my white tops. My mum insisted that I wear something with padding for 'support'. All of a sudden, I got unwanted attention and felt self-conscious. Boys liked to ping my straps. I was only 10. I struggled with needing to cover my nipples and boobs with a bra until I was 20. Now I only wear crop tops to keep breast pads in place. Bra-free for nearly four years now. Wouldn't go back.

Rebecca: My first bra was a 34C mega lacy affair after mum kind of measured me up, telling me I was getting older so needed to wear something more suitable than a crop top... the bra just appeared after her next shopping trip. Hideous itchy thing from the old persons' department I'm guessing, modesty over comfort likely her philosophy. I wore the wrong size bra until about six years ago when I stopped doing the 'back size + x' method and bought my measured size + cup that actually fitted everything in properly depending on style. I have about one cup size difference between my breasts so it can be a challenge to find something at times... I love my breasts! They have sustained my children through their first year/years of life and that makes them just plain awesome!

Eleanor: If you're a 32J, going with no bra means sweat rashes and under-boob thrush, and the ever-joyful rolling over onto your own nipple during the night. I still remember being 20 and getting really well-fitting bras for the first time (as a birthday present, because expensive!). It felt like I was actually young, instead of granny-shaped.

Rachael: I'm also booby. My dog frequently treads on my nipples when she's getting into bed with me (side sleeper)!

Viv: I don't like bras, too tight! I wear a little cotton crop top as my breasts feel the cold, ha ha! But it doesn't support them, I don't feel they need any. Much more comfy. :)

Christine: My first bra was at age 10, nearly 11, in the summer holidays before I started high school. It was a 34A taken in by my Mum to be a 34AA. I had tiny boobs but my Mum said my sticky-out nipples needed covering. It was so embarrassing wearing a bra so young. The boys used to try to ping my bra strap through my school blouse, which was mortifying. Crop tops didn't exist then. I did have some that were my size from the catalogue soon after. It was a relief from teasing once the rest of the girls caught up.

Jo: I have a sensory processing problem and find standard bras too much agony to face most days. I have some soft ones that I wear on good days, yoga ones on bad days, sports bras for working out – but they are a swine to get off without dislocating something. I have a couple of posh bras that I have for certain outfits that just don't work without, but they stay on for the bare minimum of time required. My stretchy yoga bras saved my sanity – they are reasonably priced and are big enough, which was a surprise to me.

Ann: I remember going to buy my first bra, with my mum. I was keen to get one, in order to keep up with my friends (I was the youngest in my school year by some way, and as a naturally petite kind of girl, I was never going to be ahead in the booby race!). My mum found it hilarious that her daughter who, as a young child, had been naked at any opportunity, was now willingly wrapping herself in elastic. Now, I think I only wear bras because society expects us to have immobile boobs with nipples that don't show... I always felt rather frustrated/disappointed in my boobs when I was a teenager, as I would have liked them to be bigger. Now that I have grown a child with them, I think they are simply awesome!

Nicola: Same! I always hated my boobs because my nipples weren't in the 'right place', they were big and saggy. But now I simply love them. I will be doing everything I can to let my daughter know how amazing her boobies are because of the job they do!

Laura: Love bras. I am relatively large chested and was very sporty and active when younger. So, I learnt to love them. I couldn't comfortably run around with my children now without one. It's hard to find good fitting bras if you are above a D cup, especially if you measure less than 38 across the back. Sigh.

Hannah: The general horror of being a relatively flat-chested teenager in the 1990s (relatively in that I was very slim) when there was so much attention on breasts being 'sexy'. The relief in my 20s realising it was more important to be comfortable! Now, in my 30s, having breastfed for nine months and being happily bra-free for most of it, I really don't care what anyone else thinks of my boobs.

France: When I was a teen I had two pudgy tennis balls on my chest. There was a girl in my class, let's call her Dani (not her real name), who had what I thought were amazing boobs! Proper cleavage and everything. I desperately wanted Dani's boobs. Everyone wanted Dani's boobs. She had reached the unattainable heights of a D cup. Then my own B cup tennis balls grew. And sagged. And I'd gone past a D cup, into probably an F or more, but because getting bras past a DD was nearly impossible, I endured 38DDs that were simultaneously too loose and too tight, and had that attractive four-boob look. Until I went underwear shopping in Paris. Revelation! 'But Madame is not a 100-band size, Madame is 85 at most!' And Madame was indeed an 85 (which is a 32) F. And discovered that bras had different shapes, and that the right fit on a balconette bra is really quite something! And my boobs looked better than Dani's ever had in those prim white cotton bras that were the only kind you could wear under school shirts.

Sarah: When I was at school, I was desperate to need to wear a bra, and then when it came around, I was embarrassed and too shy and wore a glorified crop top for a long time. I'm small-chested now, but used to be a really annoying 30B or 30C depending on shop, which was never in stock. It was always a hassle and I regularly wore ill-fitting bras just because they were in stock and 'close enough'. Since breastfeeding began, I've slowly become more and more aware of breast care and find myself wearing a bra less and less, just a supportive top or something, and actually feel way more confident about my body and breasts – and that weird pain I used to get in my shoulders is gone.

Sandra: I'm 52 and started wearing bras in primary school. I hated it. Most girls in Year 6 did not need a bra. In my 20s, I discovered a lingerie shop which measured you 'properly'. I was a 32D. I've steadily increased in size to a 36F! I only now wear a bra if I'm going out, never at home unless we have visitors. I think they are an unnecessary cultural norm and I can't wait to be an old lady who no longer cares and lets it all hang loose! I do wear a substantial undergarment for running, but my daughter does not. I am bigger than her, but she definitely doesn't see bras as something she should wear. She's 21 and all about 'free the nipple'. I wonder what would happen if I didn't? Would it harm my ligaments or just feel uncomfortable? Or would the jiggling just be too embarrassing? What if my boobs clapped??

Ann: I am sitting with two seven-year-olds. I've asked them what they think of bras. After the giggling stopped, their comments included: 'Not very nice', 'If your top was too big, a bra stops people from seeing your boobs'. 'My big sister wears one'. (I ask why) 'Well, all her friends at school do, so I guess that's why. She might get told off if she didn't'. We haven't got on to patriarchal society, sexualisation and the male control of the female body yet... Now they're stuffing mangetout peas down their leotards.

Kate: I've loved bras ever since my mum suggested I get one when I was 11 and I upgraded my crop tops to a triple A. By the age of 13, I was a D cup and I've always seen my boobs as one of my best features. As such, I feel a good underwire/ push-up bra gives me confidence and helps me show off one of the only parts of my body I actually really like. Nothing like a good bit of cleavage enhancement!

Lyndsey: My dad used to buy my bras. We lived in a village, had one car and he passed a shop on his way home from work so he bought them. Maybe this helped him be relaxed around me breastfeeding the twins 20 years later.

Claire: I was very amused when my four-year-old described them as booby socks!

Kathryn

Kathryn is a bra fitter who helps pregnant and new mums choose new bras. She measures them at their homes and in groups and advises them on their different options. I asked her a few questions:

How did you get started?
I work with new mums as a doula and I'm also training to be a breastfeeding counsellor. I was originally trained by the NCT charity to fit new mums for bras and when the NCT stopped offering that service, I continued as an independent fitter and got some further training. I've been running my own business for about three years alongside my other work. I'm trained to fit any kind of bra, but at the moment I'm focusing on bras for breastfeeding.

When do you normally work with a mum?
Usually they come to me after they've had babies wanting breastfeeding bras. Sometimes I see them when they are still pregnant. Most people have breastfeeding bras with clips on the straps so you can unclip them and fold the cup down for breastfeeding. But there are other kinds like ones with soft stretchy fabric you can just push out of the way. Breastfeeding bras are not usually underwired as you need to be careful not to put pressure on the breast or cause a blocked duct. It's also important a bra isn't too small. If it's a bit too big, it's not the end of the world, but too small could be squashing everything and causing discomfort.

Do mums who breastfeed always wear a bra?
Some women struggle to get a bra that's comfy or fits. They might prefer to wear a vest top. You can get ones with some built in support. Or they might just wear softer sleep bras. It can be challenging for mums to find breastfeeding bras in certain sizes. If you have a small back measurement and a large cup, it can be particularly difficult.

Do you think mums need to wear a bra?
There are conflicting views on whether not wearing a bra can cause any issues. Some articles say that not wearing a bra can mean your breasts learn to hold themselves up and support themselves. I don't know the science behind that. I think if people want to wear bras, wear bras! If they don't want to wear a bra, don't wear a bra! At the beginning, new mums often leak milk so it can be useful to have a breast pad which soaks up the milk and some kind of bra or top that holds the breast pad in place is useful.

I know you have children. Are you about to support someone thinking about a first bra?
My daughter who is nine is just starting to grow. We went out and bought some cropped vests so she has a bit more privacy when she changes for PE. She's not at the stage of needing any support yet. One day I expect we'll be going proper bra shopping. I think it might be a challenge to find something to fit her though, as there doesn't tend to be a good range of smaller sizes. That's true for smaller women too.

What were your own experiences of being fitted for a bra?
I've been fitted in a few different department stores.

It wasn't the best experience. Shops often don't sell my size, so it sometimes feels like they are trying to sell me the wrong size. Shops often try and sell you bras which are too big on the band size and too small on the cup size. Most bras seem to be designed for women who have round high breasts – like hemispheres on their chest. But that's not often how breasts are! Most boobs are not that shape. They might be ski-slope shape. They don't fit the perfect round ideal that bra manufacturers seem to have. Bras can be the wrong shape even if you try on every size! Bra sizing is often wrong because the sizing system is from a time when fabric and technology was different. We used to always add on extra inches to the band (sometimes 'plus 4') so bras weren't so uncomfortable and tight and you could breathe. But now that the fabrics used are stretchier and bras are designed differently, that shouldn't be needed. But some bra fitters are still doing it and bras end up too big in the band, and not supporting you! So really important to check you are being fitted properly.

Do you think being a bra fitter has helped you to feel more comfortable talking about breasts? What would you say to someone just developing breasts for the first time?
That's probably more to do with the breastfeeding side of my life. I spend a lot of time talking about boobs! Everyone's breasts are different. They are probably not symmetrical and that's perfectly normal. One is usually bigger than the other. Most breasts don't look like the photo-shopped, air-brushed, professionally lit breasts you see in films, on posters, on TV. There is a massive variation of normal. And breasts are designed for feeding babies. That's their primary purpose and anything else is secondary.

Writing letters

Put a ring around the one that's right for you and leave it somewhere it will be seen.

Dear mum/dad/grown-up,

I'd like to talk about bras. You've probably noticed my breasts are changing and I feel it's time to buy some extra underwear. I'm not sure whether that's a bra or a crop top or something – or even the different options you can buy. Can we go to a shop or look online and see what might work for me? *Thank you!*

Dear mum/dad/grown-up,

I'd like to talk about bras. Someone told me that I should buy a bra and I'm uncomfortable about that. I'm not sure that's the right choice for me. I don't feel it should be someone else's decision, I feel it should be mine. Not everyone has to wear a bra and there are lots of different options out there. Can we talk about it? *Thank you!*

Dear mum/dad/grown-up,

You've probably noticed my breasts are growing. I'd like to have a conversation about bras. I'm not sure whether I need one or not and I'm not sure what options are out there. Can we talk about it? Maybe you could write a note back if talking out loud is too awkward! *Thank you!*

CHAPTER FOUR

Being a grown-up

So, let's imagine you are 14 and your breasts are on their way. With each menstrual cycle, your hormones are doing their thing. Oestrogen is developing your milk ducts and getting your ovaries ready to release an egg at the same time. Then progesterone comes along in the second half of the cycle and develops your milk-producing cells – the glands at the end of your ducts. Breasts can feel different at different times of the month. Sometimes they will feel fuller and heavier and sometimes even a bit lumpy. Your breasts, as well as your womb, are getting prepared just in case a baby is on its way. When the egg passes unfertilised, your body resets for the next opportunity. That can seem a bit daft when you are only 14, but your body wants to get ready for the time when it might not seem daft.

It can feel weird when your body is getting ready to be a woman but your brain and the rest of you isn't there yet. You can look like a woman on the outside, but the world knows you aren't one. You don't feel ready to think about things like 'looking sexy', but parts of your body are starting to look like women who ARE grown-up and sexy. It can feel special to be getting closer to being grown up. You can feel more independent and you have more control over your own life.

At the same time, it can sometimes feel frightening when you don't feel ready.

What is sexy anyway and what do breasts have to do with it? You probably know that sex is the way babies are made (most of the time). However, when sex happens between two humans, it's not just about an egg joining with a sperm – that is a teeny part of the story of sex. For humans, it's much more than that. It's about people connecting and having fun and showing how they feel about each other. It happens when grown-ups want to be as close as they can possibly be. It's also enjoyable. It gives you a tingly special feeling that is exciting and comforting and relaxing all at the same time. When you care about someone, you want them to get their exciting tingly feeling and they want you to have it too. The truth is that human sex is about pleasure a lot more often than it is about making babies.

Some people believe that sex should only happen when two people are in a committed loving long-term relationship – but that's not everyone's opinion. Some people believe you should be married – but that's not everyone's opinion. Some people believe it's something that two grown-ups can choose to do for fun because it feels good and they might not be 'in love' – but that's not everyone's opinion.

People's opinions on sex are formed because of their religion and culture and the environment around them. They also come from your family's and friends' feelings about sex. At the end of the day, you'll work out your own ideas about sex when you get older. For those who think only married people should have sex, it seems wrong when other people do it. It makes them feel sad and angry. For other people, it seems sad that grown-ups have to wait until they get married.

Many people feel that the very best sex happens when two people are in love and care about each other deeply, but that doesn't mean all sex has to be like that.

For a chunk of human history – and this is still true in some parts of the world today – it was against the law to have sex with someone if you weren't married. It could mean the most severe punishment. As time has gone by, it has generally become more acceptable for grown-ups to have sex when they aren't married. If a man and a woman are having sex and they don't want the egg and the sperm to join, they can use contraception. Conception is when the egg and sperm join and 'contra' means 'against'. Contraception stops the egg being fertilised and means sex can happen for other reasons.

Breasts are about sex because sex is about the WHOLE body: lips for kissing, necks for stroking, arms for cuddling. Breasts and nipples are often part of that. There are people who think that bottoms and legs are attractive and sexy. There are people who like feet and arms, long hair, short hair, different voices, smaller breasts, larger breasts, blue eyes, brown eyes, people who are taller than them and people who look the same as them. What someone finds attractive is very individual – which is lucky, as otherwise everyone would be asking out the same small group of people and they'd be getting very sick of it! When you find someone sexy and attractive, it's the stuff on the inside that becomes more important over time – how they make you feel, their sense of humour, how they see the world. The outside shell is usually the least interesting bit about someone, but it can have a part to play in what first attracts you.

Breasts are often important in the 'what's sexy and attractive' story. In our culture, breasts are near the top of the list. Other cultures are less excited about them, but in most cultures, they seem to matter. One theory is that people are attracted to breasts because you are attracted to someone who might be the mother of your children and having breasts is part of that. I've never met anyone who thinks, 'Hey! She looks fabulous in that dress. I love the shape of her breasts. I bet she'll make great milk,' but who knows, maybe it's buried deep in there somewhere.

Even when a grown-up isn't thinking about having sex, it can still feel good to have sexy thoughts or to look sexy. When a woman goes out with her friends, it can help her confidence to feel attractive. She might wear a top or dress she likes and she wants her breasts to look good just like she wants the rest of her body to look good.

But the most important thing is that she is in control. SHE gets to decide what she wears. SHE gets to decide if she wants to wear a tight top or a loose top. SHE is in charge of her body, no one else. Some women want to be covered, and not show the shape of their breasts, because they feel more comfortable that way. Some women want to wear clothing that shows more of their body. The same woman might want to change her mind on different days. What they wear and how they show their breasts depends on how they are feeling in that moment.

One of the most frustrating things is when someone else thinks they should be able to make decisions about *your* body. Throughout history there have been rules about what women should be allowed to wear and when women don't follow those rules, society rejects them. That's something to get angry about.

If you are a grown-up and someone finds you attractive,

they can ask you if you'd like to go out and spend time with them. You can say yes or no. They must accept your decision. If you say yes, there's a long way to go until they get to kiss you or touch you and you get to decide all along the way what you are comfortable with. If someone ever touches you in a way that you don't like, you tell someone. That's not allowed. That's true when you are a grown-up and before you are a grown-up. You are in charge of your body and you say no and tell someone if you ever feel uncomfortable.

You might notice that when you start to develop breasts, or when you start to wear a bra, other people notice. You might see them looking, which can feel strange. If the looking makes you feel uncomfortable, you can say something. In the bra chapter, you'll have seen that it sometimes goes further than that and people say things. You might even meet a twerp who pings a bra strap. You do not have to put up with that. No one else has the right to comment on your body and no one else *ever* has the right to touch you without your permission. Get some help if a twerp is annoying you. Talk to your teacher or your parents. You can say to the twerp, 'You don't have the right to do that. Grow up'. It is often an immature person who does it. It might be someone who is worried about the way their own body is changing. You can feel sorry for them as well as feel angry: 'You seem to be struggling with the concept that we are all approaching puberty. If you'd like me to recommend a book you can read or direct you to further information, please ask'.

Don't think a dozen twerps are about to start commenting though. Most people don't get their bra strap pinged at any point. It's rare, but it's good to be prepared if it does happen.

You will have breasts for most of your time on the planet.

"Breasts have a lot of fat cells so when there is more fat in your body, the cells in your breasts expand."

Once you have finished puberty, they stay roughly the same for years and years. If you put on more weight, your breasts might get bigger. Breasts have a lot of fat cells so when there is more fat in your body, the cells in your breasts expand. At other times in your life, you might have smaller fat cells and your breasts might be smaller too. If you ever get pregnant and have a baby, your breasts will change again and get ready to make milk. When you've finished breastfeeding, your breasts shift back to normal grown-up 'not feeding a baby' mode.

When a woman gets older – usually around 50 years old (sometimes a bit before and sometimes after) – the menopause happens. Puberty is the body getting ready to make a baby and menopause is the time in a woman's life when her body says, 'OK, that's it for the baby-making phase of my life. Time to slow down with the hormones'. Her body makes less oestrogen and her breast tissue changes shape a bit. It might lose some of its fullness as the milk-making tissue is no longer needed. The process takes a few years and it might also mean a bit of breast tenderness and achiness. Some people think that breastfeeding can cause someone's breasts to become droopier. That's not true. Scientists have researched it. Being pregnant can change the shape of your breasts, but it's time and genetics that make the main difference. Other things can have an effect – like whether someone smokes and how someone's weight has changed over their life.

At the end of someone's life, breasts can feel like old friends. You've been through a lot together. They might have fed your babies. You've experienced periods together. You shared boyfriends (or girlfriends). They helped you to feel confident and important and at other times, they might have made you feel uncomfortable and vulnerable. Some people have cute names for their breasts. I know someone who has named hers. Some people call them their 'girls'. Here are some other words that sometimes get used: boobs, pillows, hooters, gazongas, fun bags, puppies, na-nas, baps, tits, rack, melons, headlights, charlies, dugs, Bristols, norks, chi-chis, floaties, ta-tas. That list could be a lot longer. I don't recommend telling your granny you know all those words, by the way.

Thea, 17

My mum always told me that when I would hit puberty, I was going to have bigger boobs than other girls. My nan had bigger boobs and it was a genetic thing. So, from a very young age, I was aware that might be in my future. I'm quite curvy anyway and I expected it was going to happen.

I did end up being bustier for my age group than my classmates. I remember we went to buy bras in department stores and I could only buy the simple and plain bras that gave support – this is a few years ago now. The girls in my class that were 'itty bitty small' could wear all the pretty lace ones. It felt like my transition was much more profound than it was for my classmates. I started wearing bra tops from around 10. I didn't feel I could wear nothing. When I was around 12–13, I had to start wearing proper bras.

Today, fashion is the best it's ever been. My mum says that too. She remembers being ridiculed when she was younger. There was only really one bra she could wear for bustier women and it didn't make you feel amazing or pretty. It was comfortable and practical. Now, fashion has developed so much. Online retailers have a range of nice bras and ones that help you to feel confident inside. My mum had a tough time at school. When she was younger they didn't have proper sports bras and she was really sporty.

It's not always easy going shopping. I have to look for certain shapes that fit me. I have less choice than my friends. I couldn't wear a slinky dress that might just go straight down or shows lots of cleavage. The expense is the other main thing. My friends can buy bras and bralettes for £12. I have to go to a specialised shop that sells bras for more like £30–40.

When I was younger, I lacked confidence with my breasts. I was teased and boys, who hadn't even hit puberty, were silly and might sometimes laugh. Now, I've gained more confidence. I've learned to love my body shape and it's the way I am, and I wouldn't change it for anyone else. Girls that go through puberty need that little bit of self-confidence and to have a support system, so they can talk to people. One of my best mates is just as busty as me and we talk about it all the time. We talk about being hot in the summer and how your clothes stick to you. My mum is also part of my support system. She has given me lots of advice about how to 'rock it' and be confident within yourself.

If you are changing for the first time and feeling worried, confide in people. There's no point bottling it up. If you bottle up your feelings and internalise themother people can pick up on that. People who express themselves and don't bottle things up are more likely to be confident people. If you are vulnerable, that sometimes means that stupid people are more likely to pick on you. Ask questions. Talk to your mum. Confide in people you trust. Confide in people who are in the same position as you. You are in a perfect environment at the moment. Fashion has developed. Lingerie has developed.

It's true that social media is always going to be an issue, but remember, nobody is the perfect shape. There's no such thing. One thing my mum always told me is that girls who have small boobs often aspire to bigger ones and girls who have big boobs often want smaller ones! There's always someone out there who is jealous of you. My friend at school who is smaller than me says she wishes she could wear a dress like me and have it fit on the top half. There is always someone out there who admires your shape.

When a baby is born, one of the first questions often asked is 'boy or girl?' That question is sometimes asked before the baby even comes out! We classify someone's biological sex (male or female) based on the appearance of their genitals at birth. As we grow up, for most people, biological sex is the same as gender identity. We feel that we are a boy or a girl on the inside too. This doesn't mean that we might not sometimes be confused about what it means to be a boy or a girl and want to explore what 'male' and 'female' behaviours are. It's normal to challenge what society says girls and boys are supposed to do. But for some people (perhaps 1 in 100, or some say 3 in 100), something feels different. They feel a mismatch between their biological sex and their gender identity. That feeling of mismatch isn't just a phase and it gets stronger over time. It doesn't mean a boy who wants to wear a dress or a girl who wants to be a 'tomboy' – the feelings go much deeper than that and can be very upsetting and distressing. The word 'trans' is often used to describe people whose gender identity does not match the female/male biological sex label given to them at birth.

Jack lives in Germany. When Jack was born, someone said 'it's a girl', but now Jack uses the word 'he'. He had some surgery to remove his breasts as part of his journey towards society seeing him as a 'he'. However, Jack doesn't feel his journey was about 'changing' from female to male. He explains that gender is more complicated than that.

Before he made any changes, Jack did a LOT of thinking and a LOT of talking. He knew that if he started to make changes to his body, he might never be able to go back and he wanted to be absolutely sure he was doing what was right for him. It wasn't a decision to take lightly. It took a very long time before he was able to understand what he wanted to do.

Jack, 35

My first memories of breasts are my mums. Probably her getting dressed, nothing dramatic! My older sister Becky and I were breastfed but I'm not sure how long for. When I first started to develop my own breasts, at the end of primary school, I would have described myself as a 'tomboy'. That was also how other people were perceiving me. At that time, I would have categorised myself as a girl or female and breasts arriving didn't feel like a conflict. I didn't have very large breasts and I had quite a slender figure. But I wasn't totally happy with the development.

Over the course of being in secondary school, from about 11 until 16 years, there was a gradual process when I realised this wasn't just about being a 'tomboy'. Over that period, I didn't have another label to describe myself but the tomboy thing wasn't working. I wasn't really talking to other people about how I was feeling because I didn't have the language to articulate it. It was easier to talk about my sexuality (being attracted to girls) than it was to talk about conflicts around my body or my gender. I guess I was still confused. It wasn't that I didn't have people I could talk to, I guess I just didn't really know what I would be saying if I did.

Early on, I knew the word 'lesbian' wasn't really me either. It was a problematic term and that was one of the early signs that the classification of 'females being attracted to females' didn't work for me and something else was going on.

When I was at university, at around 20 years old, I started to find the right language. I was meeting other people with different experiences and different experiences of gender. That helped me to be able to articulate what I was feeling. I met other people who had that language.

Even when I had the language, I still had a long journey with a lot of questioning and a lot of talking to different people about their experiences – on an emotional and practical level. I didn't talk to any medical professionals for a long time. I needed to take time to understand myself and my confusion and my emotions. It took a long time for me to ask myself what I wanted to do and what I felt was necessary. I needed to reflect on what I felt uncomfortable with and what could I live with and not live with.

I had a couple of concrete conversations with my family before I did any surgery or took any hormones. They were part of a long ongoing discussion about gender in general. In the first conversation, I explained I was going to change my name. I changed my name about a year before I identified as being 'trans'. Later on, we had a conversation about me having surgery and body changes. The conversation about changing my name was difficult. My first name was the one that they had given me. I was rejecting that. And at that stage, it wasn't really clear to them what my journey was going to be. It was a hard conversation but not a bad one. In the second conversation, things were more concrete. I showed them a video of a performance to do with being trans. The conversation went really well. It didn't come out of the blue. However, my parents were worried about me and my choices having an impact on my life and me being unhappy about my choices. There were worried about me experiencing discrimination.

I was living in Germany when I did decide I needed to make some bigger, more physical changes. Initially you go to a psychiatrist and they diagnose you as having 'gender dysphoria' (a medical condition). For me, this felt like a hoop I had to jump through. They write a letter which you can then take to a surgeon who will be able to operate to change your body. I decided to have my breast surgery in the USA at a private clinic. I have had a double mastectomy – which means both breasts have been removed. Some people call that 'top surgery'. I had that when I was 27. That's what I felt I needed to do.

I'm now at a point where I'm read by society as being 'male'. Sometimes this is useful. Sometimes it has its own complications. My passports and identity documents are male. Society sees me that way. It's rare these days for people to read my background as anything other than male. This can sometimes make me feel like people aren't seeing the whole 'me' and the richness of my journey. But during the period where my documents didn't fit how I was feeling and presenting, there was a constant need to clarify one way or the other. People's reactions were a factor in my decision to make permanent physical changes and to take hormones. It was a lot to do with not wanting that constant dialogue. I constantly had to talk about my background in social situations. I felt paranoid and uncomfortable. I still have complications in everyday situations due to not being 'binary' (where to go for a wee for example or getting changed in public) but I'm really happy that these problems are now much less than before.

In some way, I actually liked my own breasts. Having this surgery doesn't mean I didn't! They gave me pleasure. That's not always the experience of people who have top surgery, but it was mine. Breasts in general – definitely good! Life with breasts was not all bad for me but the balance had tipped. My breasts somehow didn't feel like mine, they didn't fit my image of myself or how I felt in my skin. I felt I needed to have this operation for me.

Before the breast surgery, in some ways, I felt sad about my breasts being removed (even now, I do occasionally). There was almost a period of mourning. I was aware of what I would be losing. But at the same time, also a feeling of excitement. Although I was saying goodbye to something I didn't actually hate, after the surgery I had a real high. I might have had incisions and bandages, but I had a sense of great relief and liberation. I know that sounds dramatic. I felt like I had thrown off a chain.

I didn't need a new wardrobe. I had been binding my breasts before the surgery (which is when you wear fabric that flattens your breasts). I had been wearing a binder for a while, so my clothing was already the right shape. On a hot summer's day, the binder meant I was wearing an extra layer. I remember being sweaty and sticky. It felt restrictive. It made me constantly aware that I wasn't happy with myself.

"I still had a long journey with a lot of questioning and a lot of talking to different people about their experiences – on an emotional and practical level. I didn't talk to any medical professionals for a long time."

I also take hormones. The routine has changed over time. Initially I was having an injection of testosterone every two weeks and at the moment, I have an injection every three months. Those injections will continue as long as I want to. If I stopped taking it, there would be some physical changes. Your voice goes deeper when you start taking hormones and that doesn't go back if you stop, but some things – like the distribution of fat and muscle and your body profile – might change.

I'm not having any other surgery at this point. I continue to see doctors for my hormones. In the future, I'm pretty sure I don't want to be a parent in the sense of being a 'primary parent' for a child. But I might meet someone who has a child. I don't know what the future might bring.

My sister has two children. To them, I am Uncle Jack. They are a bit too small to understand all the complexities of gender and any topic in a lot of depth. But when children grow up, they are able to understand that the idea of gender doesn't have to be as fixed as our society gives the impression it is. Even at quite a young age, children can understand it may not be 'binary' (one of two things). Children now have more access to the language and ways of understanding more about gender and identity. I wish I had had that more growing up.

I'm really happy I took a long time to make my decisions about what I wanted to change. Some people may have those answers when they are younger. But it's crucial that medical intervention isn't seen as 'quick fix'. It takes time to question yourself and learn about yourself. At least, it did for me. Every individual's story is different.

Our society pushes us into thinking that people who have more complicated ideas about gender have an 'illness'. I think sometimes it's the society we live in that makes us think we have to change. We aren't supported to be at peace within ourselves in the way we came into the world. It's a social problem that we should try to change – rather than seeing it as a medical condition that we can only solve with medical intervention.

Society is constructed to promote the idea that there is male, female and now there is a third group called 'trans' (and a fourth group called 'inter'). People's attitudes are changing and this helps to give all of us more options to be ourselves. But gender expression is more complicated than just creating a new label. You shouldn't have to conform to society's ideas about what gender should be or what your body should look like. More labels can sometimes just lead to more limitations. If you feel that you have to have surgery or take hormones to conform this shows that we have a long way to go before individuals genuinely feel accepted as who they are. Having breasts AND a masculine identity, for example, shouldn't have to be a contradiction!

I don't see myself as having gone from 'female' to 'male'. I don't see myself as fully male. I feel comfortable using 'he' and 'him' but I know people who have entirely rejected the idea that they have to be 'he' or 'she'.

One Canadian man called Trevor MacDonald had a story a bit like Jack's. He was born as a girl by most people's definitions and then later had surgery to change his chest and took hormones. Later, he got pregnant and gave birth (because the parts of his body that meant he could do that were still there). Even though most of his breast tissue had been removed long before he was pregnant, he was able to make some milk for his baby. He fed his baby extra milk using a tube attached to his chest so the baby could still latch onto the nipple to be fed. The extra milk used was human milk donated by other families. Trevor then trained to help other breastfeeding families (some people might choose to say 'chest feeding' if they don't feel the word breast is right for their situation).

There are not many people in the world like Jack and Trevor. But there are lots of people who feel confused while they are growing up or feel 'different' or left out. There are lots of ways to be boys and girls and it takes a long time to find out what feels comfortable – not least because society often wants to push us into boxes and tell us girls are 'supposed to' behave a certain way or boys are 'supposed to' think a certain way. It takes a long time to figure out who you really are. If you are worried about anything, talk to people you care about.

CHAPTER FIVE

Being a mother

A baby takes about 40 weeks to develop inside the mum's womb. At the beginning, they are just two cells joining together – the female egg from the woman's ovaries and the male sperm from the man's testicles. Even when they join together, they are so tiny that they can only be seen by a microscope – and that's unlikely to happen as no one is going to be able to fit a microscope inside your mum to take a look.

Do you know some babies DO start their life outside their mums? Have you ever heard of something called IVF? That means *in-vitro fertilisation*. 'In vitro' means 'in glass'. The egg and sperm are joined together by scientists in a laboratory. The very first baby created 'in glass' was called Louise Brown and she now has two children of her own and lives in Oldham in England. There are lots of reasons why a baby might start their life like that. Sometimes the mum is using sperm donated by a man she isn't in a relationship with. Sometimes a couple need medical help because they aren't getting pregnant by having sex. When the fertilisation has occurred (the bit when the egg and sperm actually join), the joined-up cells stay in the lab for a few days and then are put inside the mother to continue their life. Everyone hopes that the mini-not-quite-baby (still too small to see) will get comfy in the lining of the mum's womb and decide to stick around. When the cells have first been joined together, they are called a zygote. As they develop and get a little bigger, they become an embryo.

However the first bit happens, the next stage is inside the mum's womb. Something called a placenta grows alongside the baby. It's a chunky thing and at the end it weighs about the same as three or four apples. It doesn't look like apples though – more like a bit of meat – which is probably not surprising as that's what it is, mummy meat! The placenta joins the baby to the wall of the mum's womb. The baby doesn't have to hang on by itself, which is just as well as it has nothing to hang on with yet. The placenta is attached to the wall of the womb and the baby is joined to the placenta by its umbilical cord. The cord is connected to the baby where your tummy button is. (I bet some of you have just touched your tummy button.) The placenta and the cord give the baby the oxygen it needs because it can't breathe yet. The oxygen travels through the mum's blood. It also gives the baby the nutrients it needs to grow and have energy (all those teeny bits of sandwiches).

Week 5 Week 9 Week 14 Week 18

When a baby is four weeks old, it's the size of a poppy seed. At five weeks, it's like a sesame seed. At six weeks, like a lentil. At nine weeks, like a grape. At 14 weeks, it's about the size of a lemon. We don't call the baby an embryo any more, it's a foetus (which Americans call a fetus, they really do like saving on those Os). Parents can sign up to receive emails comparing their baby to fruit and vegetables for the entire 40 weeks if they like. (Week 37 – Swiss chard. Anyone know what Swiss chard looks like?). By the time 40 weeks comes along, people are talking about small pumpkins or a small watermelon.

Not all babies stay inside for 40 weeks. Some want to hang on for a little bit longer. Others come out sooner (that's called 'being premature'). Mature is 'fully developed'. Premature is not fully developed. Immature is that annoying person in your class who sniggers when someone wears a bra for the first time. If a baby is very early, they need to stay in hospital and be looked after by doctors and nurses (and their parents) until they are strong enough and big enough to go home.

When babies are inside, as they grow, the mum's womb grows and stretches and her tummy does too. Women aren't just carrying the weight of the baby, but also the weight of

Week 22

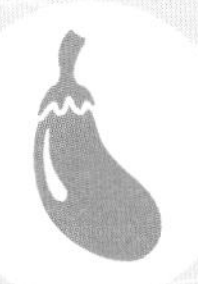
Week 28

Week 33

Week 35

the placenta (carry four apples around AND a baby) and the liquid the baby is surrounded by. The baby is in a thin sac called the amniotic sac and it's filled with protective liquid called amniotic fluid. You might have heard that when people are going to give birth, there's talk of their 'waters breaking'. The sac breaks and the liquid splashes out. On films and TV, that's usually happening as the main character is rushing to hospital and birth seems to take about 10 minutes in total. There's a splash of something on the floor and everyone notices. It real life it can take a lot longer and not all women notice when their waters trickle out.

As the baby grows, some mums have scans so they and their healthcare team can see how the baby is developing. Sometimes they have tests to check what's going on. Sometimes people even take a sneaky peak to see if they are having a boy or a girl with an ultrasound scan. They might be having twins or triplets and have both!

A mum starts to produce milk when she is about halfway through being pregnant and some mums notice that their breasts are leaking in pregnancy. Not enough to spray like a fountain, but the odd drip or some crusty yellow bits in their bra. The first milk, called colostrum, is a golden yellow colour. The pregnancy hormones have helped the breasts to develop further and get ready for the baby. Her breasts haven't changed much since she was a teenager, but when she's pregnant, they have a bit more work to do. Just like when she was a teenager, oestrogen helps the milk ducts to grow and progesterone helps the milk lobes and milk producing areas to develop. Her breasts may start to look different on the outside too. You might be able to see more of the blood vessels from the outside. The nipple and areola (the coloured circle around the nipple) may start to look darker and even change shape slightly.

Why do you think the areola and nipple are changing? Some think it could be to help the newborn baby, who has rubbish eyesight, to find it! 'Hey! The milk is over here!' But other scientists think that's unlikely as new babies often breastfeed with their eyes shut. Babies have a good sense of smell and can sniff their way to the right place too.

When a baby comes out, it can happen in a couple of different ways: either through the mum's vagina, or sometimes in a caesarean birth (what my friend calls 'out through the sun roof'), when surgeons take the baby out through mum's tummy.

When the baby is ready to come out, the mum starts feeling squeezes around her womb. The squeezes get stronger as they help the baby to move downwards towards the exit. Some babies are born in hospitals or birth centres and some babies are born at home. Everyone's birth is different. Many mothers remember it as one of the happiest experiences of their lives. Some babies need a bit of extra help to come out. Some might even need to be removed by a surgeon who carefully cuts a way out through the mum's tummy (and then carefully stitches it back up again). That's the caesarean birth.

Some women give birth in a pool of water; others walk around and listen to music. Some have their partners with them or a friend. It might take an hour or three days for a baby to make their final journey into the world.

However they come out, we want them to stay close to mum when they do. We talked before about skin-to-skin. If a baby is lying on their mum and neither of them are wearing clothes, it keeps the baby warm (more than if they were wearing a little woolly jumper). It also introduces the baby to the mum's friendly bacteria and helps the mum and baby to bond and get ready for their first feed. It is helpful if the baby does come out through mum's vagina, because the vagina is close to the end of the mum's intestines (are you with me here?) and all the friendly bacteria will be in that area. And it's extremely common for a mum to do a poo while the baby is coming out – friendly bacteria meet-and-greet! I know that might sound yucky, but scientists are learning more and more about the friendly bacteria and why they are important and they certainly aren't using the word 'yucky'. But sometimes it's decided that going out through the tummy is the best way. Mums who do have their babies taken out through their tummies need to do skin-to-skin to make sure their baby doesn't miss out on the bacteria meet-and-greet.

After the baby has arrived, it's good if they can stay in contact with mum's body. Babies can wriggle around and find the breast all by themselves if you leave them to it. Mums often help a bit too though.

You probably know that babies put their mouth around the nipple part and milk comes out. Babies aren't just sucking the nipple like someone sucking through a straw. They have a big mouthful of their mum's breast like taking a first bite of an apple (but no biting here! Not least because there's no teeth yet). The baby's tongue scoops the breast deep inside its mouth. Milk comes out because the baby is sucking but it's also about the baby's tongue doing clever things and little muscles inside mum's breasts that squeeze the milk down towards baby. And did you know the milk doesn't just come out of one hole in the middle of the nipple? Some people

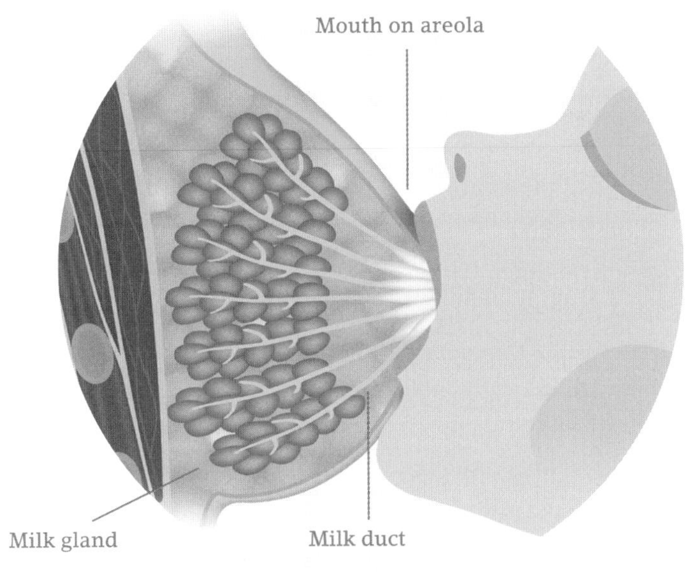

have several holes and it looks like a little shower. Most people have at least two or three holes.

Around the outside of the grape-shaped bits deep inside the breast, which are filled with milk, there are tiny muscles. It's as if the grape skin on a grape can squeeze and squash the grape inside and that action pushes the milk down to the baby. When it's time for the baby to feed, the baby latches on with a big mouthful. Their mouth is around the nipple but also on the coloured bit around the outside of the nipple, the areola. If the baby just had the nipple in its mouth, it wouldn't have enough breast and it would be hard to get the milk out. It would also start to hurt the mum, as the nipple would probably rub on the roof of the baby's mouth. Instead, the baby gets a big wedge of breast that fills their whole mouth.

Touch your tongue up onto the roof of your mouth now (I'll wait). Can you feel that at the front – just behind your top teeth – there are some ridges and hard bumpy bits and then as you go further back it feels soft and squishy? The nipple ends up near the back, pointing the milk in the right direction. We don't want the nipple to rub on the hard bit at the front so that's why so much of the breast goes in the baby's mouth.

When the baby first starts sucking, it sends some of those hormone messages to mum's brain. That tells her body that it's time to help the milk to flow. The little muscles around the outside of the grape-shaped alveoli squeeze the milk down towards the baby. The stalks of the ducts get wider and the baby can get the milk.

So, it isn't just the baby doing a suck. The mum's brain, breast muscles and milk ducts all have a part to play.

The oxytocin hormone that squeezes the muscles around the alveoli and widens the ducts also affects our feelings. Sometimes it's called 'the love hormone' because it helps us to fall in love and feel connected and bonded to people. It helps develop the relationship between a baby and its parents. It also helps squeeze the mum's womb back to being its normal size after being the shape of her baby. When someone who isn't the mum holds the baby close, they can get some of that oxytocin too. We get it even when we're older and we cuddle someone we love.

For the first few days, the mum continues to make the colostrum milk she was making when she was pregnant. The baby doesn't need to eat much as their stomach is so small. On day three after birth, their stomach is about the size of a ping-pong ball.

After a few days, the colostrum starts to change to the mature milk that will be around for the rest of the time the child breastfeeds. Mature milk is paler in colour and contains more fat and less protein and there's lots more of it. When the milk changes, a mum's breasts may feel full and uncomfortable for a couple of days. That's called being engorged. As long as she keeps breastfeeding and the baby is attached properly and has a mouthful without just being on the nipple, everything should settle down.

Babies like to breastfeed little and often. When they take out milk, it tells the mum's body to make more. The more frequently a baby feeds, the more messages the mum's breasts get. We call it a 'supply and demand' system. Breasts aren't like containers that fill and empty. They are more like little rivers or streams, where sometimes the flow is fast and sometimes it slows down, but it very very rarely dries up. In fact, when the breasts are emptier the body produces milk even more quickly than when the breast is fuller! Breasts are clever factories that make milk from the nutrients in the mum's bloodstream. A mum can continue eating normally. She can drink when she's thirsty and she may be a little bit hungrier than usual, but breastfeeding mums don't eat a ton more than other mums.

When mums eat and drink it passes into their stomach and digestive system. Then their body breaks the food down into tiny pieces (nutrients) that get absorbed into their blood stream. Some of that food will get used by the mum and some will go to the baby. The nutrients (and water) travel through mum's blood towards her breast. Breasts have a lot of blood vessels in them. There's a busy transport system of blood looking after the breasts as they do their important job. Blood surrounds the alveoli and the nutrients filter into the milk-making tissue so the milk can contain protein, fat and carbohydrates in the right amount. Protein is made from carbon, oxygen, hydrogen and nitrogen molecules in a particular combination. Fat is made from carbon, oxygen and hydrogen molecules in another combination. Starches and sugars (carbohydrates) are made from carbon, oxygen and hydrogen in yet another combination.

Do you get the sense that nature is really clever at just moving carbon, hydrogen and oxygen molecules around?!

Not all of the nutrients in breastmilk come from the food the mum ate that day or even that week. Calories in the milk can come from fat that has been on the mum's body for a while. That includes some of the vitamins absorbed in the fat. If a mum has a day when she eats a bit less, her body will make sure her milk contains what it needs. And it's OK if mums don't eat super-healthily all the time. It's better for *her* if she doesn't survive on biscuits and burgers and eats a good range of healthy foods, but her baby won't get 'bits of burger' in the milk. Baby will get the *nutrients* from the burger broken down into the important bits. The amount of fat in breastmilk isn't about whether a mum eats a lot of cream cakes or whether a mum has lots of wobbly bits. The amount of fat varies when the breast is fuller or emptier and it's at the same level for most humans.

Just like older people can have food allergies, very occasionally babies can too. Some mums control what they eat so the baby won't be getting the food components that cause them problems through their milk.

New babies want to be on the breast a lot. On some days, it can feel like they hardly want to stop, but this phase doesn't last forever. Babies feed frequently because they have little tummies and they are developing their mum's milk supply, but also because it's NICE. The milk is warm and sweet and when they are cuddling in mum's arms, it's cosy and they feel safe.

If you watch nature documentaries, gorilla babies are clinging to their mums as they amble through the jungle. Monkey babies hang on while their mums swing through the trees. We are primates too. Just like no gorilla mummy pops her baby down and goes off for ages and leaves them to it, we are designed to stick close to our mums. Breastfeeding is about cuddles and connection as much as it is about food. Breastfeeding is drinking and eating and being warm and cuddles. It's annoying that it's called 'breastfeeding' and everyone thinks it's just about the milk. It's much more than feeding.

Some mums carry their babies in slings: shaped pieces of cloth that mean they can wrap their babies close to them and carry them without having to 'carry' them. They can walk around and get other things done while babies are feeding and sleeping. It's also a lot easier to get on the bus with a baby wrapped in a sling than in a chunky big pram.

When mums give birth in hospital, they might be home the next day. Then a midwife visits them at home for the next little while to check everything is going OK and the baby is putting on weight and having enough to eat. They also want to check that the mum is feeling good after the birth.

Sometimes mums need a bit of help getting the hang of how to breastfeed. *You* already know (because you just read it!) that the baby shouldn't just have the nipple in its mouth and should be taking a big mouthful of breast, but not all *mums* get that information. Some mums don't know that it's normal for babies to feed a lot and they aren't just doing it to get milk but to feel safe and cosy. If their babies want to feed again after only an hour, they worry that something might be wrong.

If the baby is just on the nipple, they won't get enough breast in their mouths and it can start to get sore for the mums. They might need to hold the baby a bit differently. Sometimes the baby isn't close enough. Perhaps the baby's chin isn't touching the breast? Perhaps the baby's arm is in the way or some bunched-up clothing is pushing baby away? Maybe the baby is too low or too high and the nipple is being pulled in the wrong direction? Maybe the mum is trying to hold the weight of baby's head and body just on her arms and hands and she's getting tired and the baby is slipping off? It usually works better if the baby is supported. Maybe mum can lean back so the baby is supported by her whole body? Some mums use cushions and pillows to support the baby.

If things don't quite feel right, a mum's midwife can help, or her health visitor (a nurse who helps new families). Or the mum might visit a breastfeeding drop-in group and talk to a breastfeeding peer supporter or a breastfeeding counsellor or a lactation consultant. They might also call a helpline and talk to someone who can help on the phone.

I'm a breastfeeding counsellor and a lactation consultant. That means I talk to mums a lot about how breastfeeding is going and I help them by sharing information and supporting them to work out why things aren't going to plan. I speak to people on the phone and at groups where people come with their babies and I see people in their homes. It took me several years to train to be a lactation consultant but even if people only know a few simple things – like 'the baby's chin should be touching your breast' or 'your nipple shouldn't come out of the baby's mouth looking squashed' – they can make all the difference.

Usually it takes a few days for new parents to get the

hang of breastfeeding. It can take a little while to recover after the birth and mums need some looking after. Dads and partners and other family members are a really important part of the breastfeeding story because new mums need help. If the other parent knows how breastfeeding works and can be supportive it makes a huge difference. After a while, mums might learn how to breastfeed lying down so they can rest while they're feeding. They get better at recognising when baby wants to breastfeed and they start to feel more confident.

Of course, breasts aren't see-through, so you can't see the milk being made and you can't measure what's coming out just by looking. We live in a society where we like to measure things and breasts don't come with little lines showing millilitres on them. Luckily, you can tell how much baby is getting in other ways. Babies have a useful display system which changes colour according to how much milk they are getting in the early days – it's called doing a poo!

New parents are taught that a baby's poo starts out sticky and black (as they've only been swallowing the fluid that surrounds them in the sac in the womb). Once they start to take in more milk, their poo gets paler. By around day four after birth, the baby's poo is often soft and yellowy. Breastfed babies have poo that smells quite sweet. Some people say it smells like a biscuit! Don't panic if you are asked to help change a nappy. It might not be as bad as you are expecting. That's because all those friendly bacteria living in a breastfed baby's gut stop their poo smelling like grown-up poo.

The baby has heavy wet nappies that tell you lots of milk is going in and the pee is coming out, and if a baby has six heavy wet nappies in 24 hours after around day four, that's a helpful sign. We weigh the baby to tell us how much milk they are getting too. It's normal for a newborn baby to lose a bit of weight for the first few days, but we don't expect them to lose any more after the colostrum changes to mature milk. We expect them to keep putting weight on regularly and in the UK, parents are given special red books to record what a baby weighs and to check they are putting enough on for their size.

Just like with adults, some babies are naturally smaller and some are bigger. They don't have to all put on exactly the same amount of weight, just what's right for them. We can also look at what the baby is doing when they are attached to the breast and we should notice their chin moving as they do deep swallows. We'll often hear swallows too (though less so when the milk changes to being fattier and thicker). Milk isn't always the same. I mentioned earlier that it changes from day to day. It can also change from minute to minute! Sometimes it might be more watery; if a baby is feeding for longer it can change to be thicker and fattier. We let babies stay on the breast as long as they need to rather than measuring how long a feed should be with a clock. That way they will get the right amount of thinner and fattier milk.

As the weeks go by, mums continue breastfeeding their babies, chatting to midwives and health visitors, getting support from their friends and family, trying not to eat only chocolate biscuits and watching some TV. Babies might wake up at night for a long time, so it can be important to try and have a nap when the baby sleeps in the day. Hopefully there are friends and family around who can help when things feel tough. It's not an easy thing to do alone – look after a baby. You might think they are fairly small and sleep all the time so how hard can it be? But mums are tired, feeling responsible for another life and having to learn lots and lots of new things. Lots of people seem to have opinions about how they should be doing things and not all of those opinions are helpful!

It's magic and wonderful and amazing and tiring and tough and awful all at the same time. That's not true of many things. Maybe like climbing Mount Everest if you are someone who really wants to climb Mount Everest?

Not every mum just feeds their baby with the breast. Some mums take out the milk using a machine called a breast pump or sometimes by squeezing with their hands (we call it 'expressing'). Breast pumps don't take out milk in exactly the same way a baby does, but most mums can switch on the machine for a few minutes, pop the funnel-shaped plastic bits over their nipples and areola and the machine

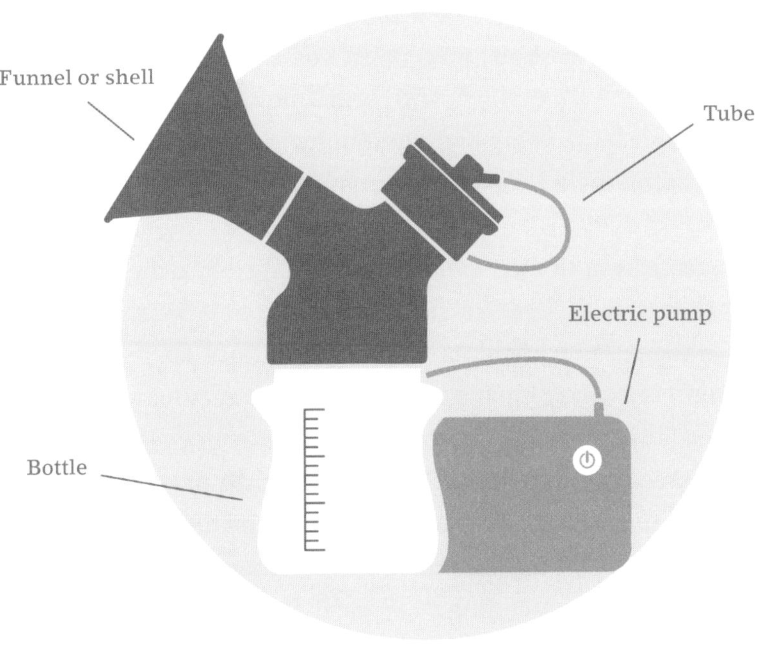

creates suction that helps the milk to come out. We still need the mum's body to release the hormone that squeezes the muscles around the milk storage areas, and some mums find it easier to trick their body into thinking the pump is a baby than others! If they pump, they can then put milk in a bottle or in a cup and a baby could have the milk that way. A mum might do that if she found it sore to breastfeed or her baby had a medical problem which meant they couldn't latch onto the breast properly. Sometimes mums do it because they want to make sure their baby is getting extra milk while they are sorting out how to breastfeed. Sometimes a midwife or a nurse might suggest a baby is given a bit of extra milk to help them put on weight. Or maybe a mum has to leave the baby for a while and someone else will be giving the milk.

Often if mums need to go back to work when they are still breastfeeding, they will take a pump to work and have a break to take some milk out. Their baby can have that milk when they are at work the next day. I wonder how many times you've sat on a train or a bus with someone who has a breast pump in their bag? Some breast pumps are run by batteries or by plugging them in. Some are manual – so you just move a plastic bit backwards and forwards with your hands.

Most mums in the UK start breastfeeding when their baby is first born, but not everyone. For some mums, it doesn't feel right for them. They might have read the things that scientists say about breastfeeding and human milk but decided that they'd prefer to feed their baby in another way or perhaps only do some breastfeeding. Some mums might have had a medical problem which makes breastfeeding difficult. Or they might be taking a medicine which they can't take when they are breastfeeding.

Most medicines are OK to continue taking when you are breastfeeding. Sometimes a tiny amount of the medicine might go into the baby, but it's not something that will cause them any problems. If there is a problem, you can often take a different type of medicine that does the same job so it's safe for breastfeeding. There are a small number of medical treatments that you can't have while you are breastfeeding so a mum might stop breastfeeding for a while or have to stop completely. Very, very rarely they may never be able to start.

A few generations ago, if a woman didn't breastfeed, she could find a nurse or a family member to breastfeed her baby instead. People had a job called being a 'wet nurse'. Kings and queens were usually fed by wet nurses and it was common for rich families to have someone else look after and feed their child. Sometimes royal babies went to live in separate households and didn't see their parents for months at a time! How do you think those babies felt when their wet nurses went away at the end of breastfeeding and never came back? Being a wet nurse wasn't necessarily a happy experience for the woman either. You might have left your *own* baby to look after someone else's. Poor and exploited women were often used by families who had money and control. In America, when slaves from Africa were kidnapped and being kept prisoner, African women often had to care for the babies of their white 'owners' instead of being allowed to look after their own babies.

In the 21st century, women who are unable to breastfeed might still use someone else's milk. There aren't as many wet nurses around as there used to be, but women do share milk for their babies in other ways. It's called milk donation. There are motorbikes whizzing all over the country delivering human milk to babies in hospitals who need it. Babies who are born early or who are ill do better when they have human milk to drink. If their mums aren't able to pump enough, the baby might get milk from a donor. Lots of mums breastfeed their own babies and then use a breast pump to take out some extra milk which they store in the freezer. Every now and again, a motorbike shows up at their house and the courier whisks their frozen milk away to a milk bank where it's tested, prepared and stored ready to be given to a different baby who might not be able to have just its own mum's milk.

Some mums who don't breastfeed give their babies a milk called 'formula' as their main food. Formula is made by different companies from lots of different ingredients to give the baby vitamins and minerals and nutrients. The protein and fat in formula is mostly made from cow's milk. There are also ingredients from plants and other animals in a careful balance, but there's only a tiny fraction of the ingredients that are in breastmilk. You can buy formula in a powder, which you then mix with hot water to make a liquid milk. Or you can buy it in a carton where it's already a liquid, which costs a bit more. There are regulations that say what manufacturers have to put in the formula, because if something important is missed out, or something extra added in that hasn't been tested, it could be very harmful for babies who are relying on it.

Some mums breastfeed and use their own pumped milk but also sometimes give formula. Babies can't drink normal cow's milk until they are a year old. The cow's milk that you might use with your cereal isn't safe for babies to have as their main drink. So if a mum isn't going to give her baby breastmilk, she has to buy the formula milk made for young babies.

Some mums who give formula prefer it to breastfeeding and feel it's the right choice for their baby. It might be that breastfeeding was a struggle and making them sad. It might be that they didn't start breastfeeding in the first place. Some mums are upset that they couldn't give their baby just their own milk and that their baby might be missing out on some of the ingredients that help fight disease. They might have found breastfeeding difficult to manage, or they didn't get the support they needed. Others are happy to use formula milk. Every family should get the support of their midwife, nurses and doctors to feed their baby in the way that they feel is best.

Babies drink just milk for the first six months of their life. If they eat food too early, they might not be able to digest it properly and it might also cause them health problems. After about six months, their bodies are ready. But babies aren't eating roast chicken and roast potatoes with peas and carrots followed by cherry pie and ice cream from day one. It takes a bit of time to build up to having more than one meal a day and all through the first year, milk is very important. Gradually, as they eat more solid food, less and less milk is needed. As the child gets older and takes smaller amounts of milk, mum's breasts will get signals to produce less milk and eventually, after a few weeks of no milk being removed at all, production stops completely. The milk-producing cells in the breast fade away until they might get needed in the future and then they'll wake up again with any future pregnancy. We'll talk more about when breastfeeding ends in the next chapter.

Lucy, 32

I never thought very much about my breasts until I started breastfeeding – which is strange really because I really didn't like the rest of my body until after I had children. For some reason I didn't have strong feelings either way about these slightly floppy, wobbly squidgy bits on my chest. I remember feeling annoyed that I couldn't make them push together to make a cleavage like my sister, and I remember how much I hated bras when I started wearing them – but my breasts themselves… they were just sort of hanging out there not causing me a whole lot of bother really.

Then I had a baby and suddenly my breasts were REALLY IMPORTANT. They were supposed to feed this tiny little human who screamed a lot, and sadly for me, breastfeeding hurt so I didn't really want to do it as often as my baby needed me to. All of these midwives and doctors wanted to look at my boobs and touch them, and they were huge and full of milk and sore, and although I hadn't noticed them much before I was quickly aware that I did consider my breasts to be private and now they weren't anymore. I found the pain really difficult so I stopped breastfeeding. Then I decided to try again a few weeks later. That was when I started to feel a bit more respect for my breasts. Here's the thing – when you stop breastfeeding, it takes a lot of time and work to start again. The milk goes and you have to use a breast pump many times a day to get it to come back – and it can take months to do it. But my breasts – well, they got the message and started to make milk again pretty quickly. I was so in awe of how my body could feed my baby even though I told it to stop and then changed my mind.

> "I was so in awe of how my body could feed my baby even though I told it to stop and then changed my mind."

My breasts did that – they nourished and grew my baby, and then when I had my second baby they nourished and grew him too even though he couldn't latch to my breast for four months, so I had to express for him using a breast pump while we worked out how to help him to breastfeed. I think it's amazing how my breasts could make enough milk to feed him even when I had to use a pump to get that milk out! I went on to train to help families to breastfeed as a lactation consultant, and during my training I learned so much about how breasts make milk under all sorts of difficult circumstances, and as I learned I realised that I was more and more impressed with my breasts. So now I think about my boobs quite a lot, and I think they are so totally amazing for how they kept my babies alive and growing after they were born – AND helped to soothe them when they were sad or scared or just wanted to feel really close to their Mummy. I mean – how could I NOT love them for doing that?!

CHAPTER SIX

Who makes the rules?

The way we think and talk about breasts can be confusing in our society. Breasts are seen as sexy and empowering women, but at the same time they are meant to be private and not-talked-about.

AND They seem to give us strength but also at times make us feel vulnerable.

AND Why are men showing their nipples on the beach, but women are not?

AND Why are bikinis OK at the beach but not at the playground? Is it about the sand? Being near the coast? Why is it OK to show most of your breasts then, but not in the queue at the supermarket?

AND Why is it OK for a baby to drink human milk, but a four-year-old 'should' drink cow's milk?

Where do all these 'rules' *come* from??

It can sometimes feel like there are all these rules about breasts but nobody wants to talk about what the rules are.

A woman might go to an important party where she is shaking hands with the prime minister and the queen and she is wearing a low-cut top. She could be wearing a dress that shows the shape of her breasts (and even the skin at the top of her breasts or her cleavage where her breasts touch together). This is dressing smartly. But if she showed the same amount of skin at a job interview, people would think she was a weirdo. Sometimes the rules make very little sense and they aren't rules men have to worry about!

Breasts are part of us in the same way our shoulders and our knees and our big toes are part of us. It seems society wants to see them sometimes, but only in certain ways. It is rare for a woman with larger breasts to wear a tight t-shirt without a bra. If she did, her breasts would move around. They might jiggle as she walks or leans forward. You'd be able to see the shape of her nipples through her clothes. If it was cold, her nipples might stick out even more. Just the idea of that makes people snigger. If a woman with large breasts, a tight t-shirt and no bra got on a bus, you could be sure that people would notice. They might even nudge each other or whisper something. Some people on that bus would feel really uncomfortable. But if the same woman got on the bus with her breasts in a neat bra – no movement, no nipples showing – same breasts and same woman, they wouldn't blink.

Hopefully that woman would feel strong enough to do what feels right for her. She could have lots of reasons for wanting to wear a t-shirt and no bra, but honestly, she'd have to be a little bit brave because of our society's rules. And this is in a modern world where women are prime ministers and there's nothing girls can't do. Is that fair?

Women are often judged if they show too much of their breasts, but at the exact same time, social media posts where women highlight their breasts get the most 'likes' and attention. Women are still often valued for what's on the outside and not what's inside. Breasts are everywhere, but we rarely talk about what they are really for.

This mess can make life hard for new mums. On the one hand, we know that human milk is great for human babies and we want to support new mums who are breastfeeding, but new mums often struggle to find the information they need. New mums are told breastfeeding is a good thing when they are pregnant, but when they were growing up breastfeeding was hardly talked about.

Girls might go for years just thinking about breasts as the bumps that go in bras and then all of a sudden you're expected to understand what nature designed them for and be confident about using them for their purpose – feeding babies. It can take quite an adjustment. That's why some scientists and doctors think we should be talking about breastfeeding as part of the school curriculum years before people think about having their own families. Then we come back to the problem that (snigger, giggle, chuckle) it means talking about BREASTS. Perhaps we have to get over the embarrassment part if it means that future mums and babies will be helped.

It's just as well no one decided that EYES were the sexy bit of our body that had to be hidden away and never seen when you walk around in public, as we'd all be wearing very dark sunglasses and bumping into things on cloudy days.

NEWSFLASH

It's possible for breasts to be sexy and sometimes private AND be for feeding babies at the same time. Just like it's possible for mouths to be used for eating and for kissing and sometimes for holding pens. Our body parts are often multi-purpose. BUT the feeding babies bit needs to come first whenever that's going to be helpful. If we think 'sexy first', babies and mums will suffer.

Imagine you are a new mum and your baby is just a few weeks old. You want to leave your home (which doesn't happen very often) and you want to go to a café and meet a friend. You've been breastfeeding at home up until now. You've been on your sofa, with sometimes a cushion for support. Now you've got to breastfeed in a café with other people around and you don't even know what the chair is going to be like. Never in your whole life have you gone into a café and unbuttoned your shirt and taken your nipple out, but that's what you are about to do for the first time. That might feel a bit scary.

Of course, your baby doesn't know any of that. As far as they are concerned you are still exactly the same and even though the room might seem a bit different (not that they know what a 'room' is) and there are different smells and noises, they still want to feed when they are hungry and get comfort from breastfeeding. In fact, many would say your baby has a right to breastfeed and *you* have a right to go and meet your friend for a drink in a café.

Luckily, the law agrees with you. In the UK, it's against the law to ask someone to stop breastfeeding in a public place. If a café worker said, 'We'd rather you did that in a different room', they could be in serious trouble. That doesn't mean it doesn't still feel a bit scary for the mum though.

Let's imagine when you get there, and your baby wriggles around and asks for food, it just takes a moment to unbutton and pop them on. It was a lot easier than you were expecting. Having your friend there helped. They lent a hand by rolling up your jacket and putting it under your arm to support the baby's head. Once a baby is feeding, no one can see any part of your body you don't want them to. Your baby's head covers all the bits you might be worried about. From another table, you just look like someone holding a baby. Often someone gives you a warm smile and you sometimes even get a free drink!

But what if your baby was a little bit older? How would it feel if the mum was feeding an older child from her breast?

When do you think babies stop drinking human milk? Let's start with another question. Do you know any adults that drink milk from an animal? Does anyone you know put cow's milk on their cornflakes or in their coffee? Is it weird for a three-year-old to have a milkshake made from cow milk? Do you think that's wrong?

I'm guessing not.

Is it weird for a three-year-old to have human milk to drink? Is it weird for a four-year-old to have human milk to drink after they've finished school for the day? Is it OK for them to drink it from a cup? Is it OK for them to drink it from their mum?

A lot of people in the UK feel uncomfortable with that idea. Who makes those rules? Who decided it would be fine for a

BROCA

four-year-old to drink milk from a mummy who says 'moooo' and lives in a field and is a different species, but not a mummy who is their ACTUAL mummy?

I don't have the answer about who made the rules. I do know that nature doesn't quite support them though. If we look at our closest relatives, the primates (I'm not saying your family are gorillas), and compare ourselves to them – what do we learn? An anthropologist (someone who studies humans and human behaviour) called Katherine Dettwyler did a study of all the non-human primates who share more than 98% of our DNA. She looked at things like when they get their first teeth, when they can start having babies themselves, how long they live and how long they are pregnant for. She found that most non-human primates end breastfeeding when their babies get their first permanent molar (back) teeth. For humans, this would be around six years of age. One study showed that breastfeeding ended when primate babies had reached about a third of their adult weight. This happens in humans at about 5–7 years old. Looking at all the science, she thinks humans would naturally wean (the word for ending breastfeeding) between two and a half and seven years old. We start to lose our 'milk teeth' when we are around six years old. Perhaps that's nature giving us a clue?

That doesn't mean that everyone MUST be breastfed for that long. Not all mums would want that (and some didn't breastfeed even a small baby), but there are mums and toddlers who are happy to carry on breastfeeding. The health benefits don't just disappear when a baby gets a bit older. In fact, there's some evidence to suggest that nature is super clever and when an older child starts moving around and sticking disgusting things in their mouth, the bacteria-fighting ingredients rev up even more, ready to deal with the new challenge.

Human milk still contains antibodies and fats and proteins and vitamins and minerals after many years. An older child will need to eat other food – it's not like when they were a baby and the milk could provide everything they needed – but human milk is still valuable. It's also comforting as well. Some toddlers like to breastfeed before they fall asleep or when they feel upset or scared. Older children often breastfeed less frequently and, towards the end, they might only do it once or twice a day. They might even skip a few days. It doesn't mean milk is sitting inside mum 'getting old'. Breastmilk is always fresh because mum's blood that surrounds the alveoli is constantly filtering and making new milk.

Mums would like to be able to breastfeed for as long as it feels right for them, and if society says milk from a cow is better than their human milk made with antibodies that fight disease, they are not very impressed. The health organisations officially support mums who want to breastfeed for longer. On the NHS website, it says that the World Health Organization recommends that babies are breastfed for up to two years or longer. It still doesn't mean that you see many mums feeding their two-year-olds in the local coffee shop. Perhaps things will be different – and mums will feel more comfortable – when you are older and a parent yourself.

If you do see a mum breastfeeding outside the home, you can be the one to give them a warm smile. It might be that it's the very first time they are doing it and your smile will be one they remember for a very long time. It might help them to feel more comfortable the next time. You'll be doing a little bit to help that mum make her own rules.

But even when mums are just feeding little babies at home *on their own sofa*, they sometimes feel like there are 'rules' and that can be annoying. Small humans like to come and hang out at the breast for lots of different reasons. They might be hungry or thirsty or perhaps they just want a special cuddle. But some people think that babies are supposed to only feed every three or four hours and it's all about milk and nutrition. They think cuddles should be limited. Why?

Well, when your granny was a new mother, mums were often told that's how things were supposed to be. They were even told it was 'wrong' to hold a baby too much. So sometimes, when they become a new granny and meet a baby again after many years, they are still concerned if a baby feeds 'too much', even though the baby is super healthy and doing really well and the baby's mum doesn't mind at all. So it's not just the new parents who need to learn about caring for a baby, but the people around them too. Grannies might not even have breastfed their own babies and they are now seeing it for the first time.

The government has put some protection in place to make sure that mothers aren't pressured to give up breastfeeding before they really want to. The government thinks breastfeeding needs some protection to get a fair chance. Some of the companies that make formula milk are among the richest companies in the world. They have a lot of money to spend advertising their products and encouraging new families to try them. They make more money if people don't breastfeed. They say in their advertising that they know breastfeeding is the best choice for babies, but the government still feels mums need protection from their messages. Do you think it would be fair if an advert said, 'You should stop breastfeeding now! Come on! Don't be daft! Why don't you try our formula milk?' The Advertising Standards Authority would not let that happen.

It's against the law for a company that makes formula milk to advertise to a brand-new mum and encourage her to use their product instead of breastfeeding. The government has that law because they believe it helps all of us when more babies are breastfed. It means fewer babies getting ill and fewer babies going to hospital (which costs us money as our taxes have to pay to look after them) and it also protects mums, as when mums breastfeed for longer they are protected against some health conditions and they are less likely to get breast cancer, for example. It doesn't stop families using formula milk if they need or want to, but it means a decision can be made free from advertising pressure and not because a company has encouraged them to.

It might be that the *only* time you've seen breastfeeding on television was in an advert from a company that makes money when someone stops. Their aim is not to make you think, 'Oooh breastfeeding! I want to do that!' Their aim is to make you think buying their formula milk is a good idea. They might show a picture of someone breastfeeding in isolation inside her house, but the families who use formula are walking on the beach in the sunshine or with friends in a park. The companies might say they have been researching breastmilk, which might make it sound like they are using the same ingredients, but even the cleverest scientists in the world can't work out a way to copy all the ingredients in breastmilk.

Formula milk is an important product. We are lucky to have something to feed babies who don't get breastmilk. Mums who buy formula milk (whether it's from the beginning or later on when they stop breastfeeding) need support too, because being a new mum is tough for everyone. However, it's not the companies that are focused on making money that should be the ones to control the information new parents get. New parents should get support and information from their doctors and midwives and health visitors. And the doctors shouldn't only get *their* information from the companies. Some mums who use formula milk don't like that there are controls around the way formula is advertised, but most people appreciate that there are reasons why those controls are in place. Companies can't always be trusted to behave fairly when they are trying to make money.

It's always a good idea to have a questioning mind when it comes to advertising. What is this company trying to tell me? What are they trying to get me to buy? How are they trying to get me to behave? Most people think that adverts don't work on them, but companies spend millions and millions of pounds because they know that's not true. They are planting seeds in your head that tell you things about what you need and what you might be missing.

Often you don't even know the seeds are there. It might not always be obvious that someone is trying to sell you a product. Sometimes a celebrity might post on social media wearing certain clothes or make-up and trying to promote an image. They are saying, 'Don't you want to look like me?'. They might not hold up a sign saying, 'This is the best lipstick', but they are advertising in a different way. Companies have paid them money to use their products.

> "Photos are often changed with computers... Spots are taken away. Legs are made to look longer. Tummies are made to look flatter."

And they very often pay people who have certain body shapes and breast shapes.

Companies want to make you feel like you are missing something. If they can make you feel like you're not 'good enough', maybe you will buy their product to make you feel better. For a long time, women have been encouraged to worry about the way they look – including how their breasts look. Companies show you photos of other people that look how *you* are 'supposed to'. However, the photos you see online and in magazines AREN'T REAL. That woman DOES NOT LOOK LIKE THAT IN REAL LIFE. The photos are often changed with computers ('photoshopping' or 'airbrushing'). Spots are taken away. Legs are made to look longer. Tummies are made to look flatter. Breasts are changed so they look rounder or bigger or look the same size. Even ordinary people, who are not celebrities, are using apps to change their faces and their bodies on their social media accounts. And if you have a phone and you have social media, all these lies are filling your brain. You can be the cleverest person in the world, but advertising is finding us, whether we are looking for it or not.

Jameela Jamil is an actress and television presenter and writer and she says, 'If you have a problem with the way that I look, that is your problem, not my problem'. She describes how social media can be 'toxic' and dangerous. She started a social media campaign called 'I weigh' and instead of women talking about the shape of their bodies, they talked about what was really important: being kind, being great at their jobs, being a good friend, being a great aunt, making the most of life and learning and succeeding and finding what makes you happy. Your true weight is the value you bring to the world and how you live your life and treat others, not your actual weight in kilograms. She was contacted by a woman who was about to be made the mayor of her town. She had achieved her career and political ambitions (and was obviously clever and well-respected and had lots to celebrate), but she was worried she might look fat on her inauguration day. *That's how messed up this is*. The very cleverest women have been made to feel that they aren't good enough and their appearance is more important than who they are inside.

Breasts have been used a lot in adverts over the years. Women wearing revealing clothing or bikinis used to stand next to cars or boats so people would be excited about buying the cars or the boats. (Boats?! How random is that?) Adverts in magazines and on billboards and on television have used breasts for a long time. And I do mean breasts – quite often an advert might not even show a woman's face. She might have a perfume bottle sitting between her breasts and that's the only part of her body showing. The advert doesn't care if she has a friendly face, a university degree or even the ability to design and make fabulous perfume. Her breasts are being used as objects separate from her.

Breasts have been used to sell beer, chocolate, chicken, cosmetics, fashion, restaurants, beds, holidays and films in the last few years alone. In Moscow, Russia in 2014 a truck placed a big advert on its side which featured a pair of breasts (again, no head). 517 traffic accidents occurred that day and 'distraction' because of the advert was blamed. You can see that people want to look. That's probably why advertisers have used the breasts! But how does that make women feel? What messages does it send about how society values women's brains and skills and value as whole human beings?

A few years ago, one of the bestselling newspapers in the UK had a woman showing her breasts on page three every day. She wasn't even selling a product. She was just there – for fun. Imagine being in a café and a man was reading a newspaper at the table next to you openly looking at a huge picture of a naked woman. Women (and the men that support them) decided they had had enough and a campaign was launched. Politicians went into the Houses of Parliament wearing a t-shirt that said, 'No more page 3' and eventually the newspaper stopped it. It wasn't just because of the campaign, but because society is increasingly uncomfortable with the idea that women should be seen as bits of their bodies and not equals.

If you buy fashion magazines, you'll still see some naked women – and these are magazines that women read. There are naked women advertising watches, jewellery, perfume and skincare and mineral water this month alone. Models who are showing off expensive clothes might sometimes show their breasts, but there are also articles in the magazines that celebrate important things that women have done and lots of focus on women's brains as well as their looks. We might hear more about women's achievements, but there are still magazine covers in the newsagent focused on what someone looks like in a bikini and which social reality star has been on a diet. Things might be better in some ways, but women are still often defined by their appearance (breasts included). A famous actress is being interviewed about her work and she is photographed wearing jeans and a bra leaning against a white wall. Just a bra on top. Is that how you wander around your local High Street?

How many famous actresses do you know that aren't 'beautiful' by most people's standards? Even when they are running around saving humanity from dinosaurs or living on a spaceship in the year 2500, they are pretty. We've come a long way, but the way we look still seems to matter a lot. I told you earlier that loads of women have breasts that are different sizes. Have you ever seen a picture in a magazine or on a website of someone with differently-sized breasts? Know any famous actresses? Not all women in adverts these days are skinny, and lots of companies are starting to show larger

envy
L'AQUA
L'AQUA

> "When we see breasts used to sell perfume (and not even a whole person, just a part of them), let's say something."

women, but even then, their breasts are even and round and not wobbly and you can't see nipples. We still have to fit the ideal of what breasts should supposedly look like.

The world only gets better for women when we speak up and get angry and complain. When we get angry, we can change the world. The suffragettes who fought for women to get the vote got angry. The women who fought for the newspaper to get rid of page three got angry. If you feel something needs to change, you have the right to get angry.

When we see breasts used to sell perfume (and not even a whole person, just a part of them), let's say something. If a woman wants to choose to take off her clothes, that's her right, but let's say something when a company advertises chicken with a pair of breasts (human breasts, not chicken breasts). I'm going to be worried about a company that has so little faith in their own product that they try and distract people with a pair of breasts.

The more we use breasts to advertise and the more we say, 'pretty women have breasts like this', the harder it is to be a normal woman who might have breasts that are a different size, or have nipples that stick out, or have breasts that look a different shape from the ones we see in magazines or on Instagram. It also makes it harder to be a mother who wants to use breasts for their purpose. If breasts are just about 'sexy', it's harder to make them about milk and babies.

It can be good to get angry. Get angry if someone pings your friend's bra strap and it makes her uncomfortable. Get angry if someone judges someone just because of the shape of their body. Get angry if someone cares more about the way you look than who you are inside. Get angry if someone 'likes' a social media post where you are wearing pretty clothes but not when you are sharing clever ideas. Get angry if the shops don't make clothes that fit you and think just because you are a girl, you have to wear certain colours or certain styles. Get angry if someone on Instagram puts up a photo that isn't real and pretends that's how real bodies look. What do you feel angry about?

Noush, 22

What are your first memories of breasts?
The first thing I remember about breasts is being in the changing rooms at the start of summer before swimming at primary school in Year 5. Everyone getting changed and everybody commenting on everybody else; some people having well-developed breasts already, others just starting and some people just having completely flat chests. No one knew what was normal as we had not yet had sex education as that was at the end of Year 6. My breasts were starting to develop at this point and my period also started at around the same time.

What do you remember when your breasts started developing for the first time?
The first thing I noticed was my areolas swelling, then breast tissue started to appear slowly. I remember one breast

appearing much bigger than the other but I never properly noticed until I went for my first bra. I remember my breasts especially around my areolas being quite itchy and the whole area tender but I don't remember it lasting that long. I remember wearing a bra-vest probably until halfway though Year 6.

How do you feel about bras?
Initially I found bras really uncomfortable. I remember getting some cheap t-shirt bras which didn't fit me properly. I remember the wire digging into me on my larger breast side and my smaller side was just rubbing against my chest underneath my breast as it was not filling out the cup. After a few days of this, I remember my mum taking me and getting me fitted properly. Bras were much more expensive, but it was so worth it. I remember getting a bra that I could take a small air pocket out one side and leave it in on the other side so both breasts fitted the bra comfortably and properly.

Did people behave differently towards you once you had breasts? Did anyone make you feel uncomfortable?
I remember jealousy forming at school mainly with the girls that didn't have any and much more attention from the boys, but that was more at the end of Year 6 start of Year 7 after we had had sex education.

Do you feel social media puts any pressure on young women about how they are supposed to look?
MASSIVELY. Not so much when I was getting breasts, but I remember at secondary school Facebook wasn't the in thing and wasn't a massive part of our day-to-day life. Watching my

brother grow up three years below me at the same point, I was shocked at how quickly the girls in his year had grown up, wearing revealing clothes with their breasts on show, drinking, dressed like they are in their mid-20s caked in make-up. I think this is much to do with the bras and fashion out at the moment. I can't walk into a shop without the majority of it being crop tops and mini-skirts. I find it really worrying when I get my ID checked at 22 with two children getting my shopping on a Saturday night and there are a couple of young girls not getting their ID checked when they are under 18.

What's great about breasts?

What isn't great about breasts? They can create milk and give your child nutrition for six months, in some cases longer. They can build the most amazing bond between you and your child and knowing you're giving them what they need is the most amazing feeling.

Is there anything else you think a girl aged 9–14 needs to know about the world of breasts?

No breasts are the same, they differ from person to person. Don't judge your breasts by theirs. Their breasts would look silly on you as you are not them. You are beautiful in your own right whatever your breasts look like, big or small, odd or the same.

Lia, 15

My first memories of breasts are my mum breastfeeding my younger sister and talking about 'mummy milk'. I must have been three or four years old. My own breasts came quite early – about Year 4 or Year 5. I remember getting those white crop tops, but I wasn't sure I wanted them. We went to the shop and I felt quite embarrassed and unwilling to buy them in front of anyone. In the school PE lessons, we all had to change in the classroom in front of each other and I was the first one with the crop top on. I used to turn around to change so no one could see.

I was quite an early developer and I had actual bras by about Year 6. It was a struggle to find clothes I was comfortable wearing. Most dresses and summer clothes assumed someone my age would be an A or a B cup. Shirts with buttons had a gaping hole in the middle. I'm at an all-girls school so at least a gap in my school uniform shirt isn't that awkward.

I'm 15 now and I'm 34E. I do end up wearing old lady bras, but my friends can wear bralettes or lacy things that look a bit nicer. I have to wear bras with more support. If I want to buy a bra that has support and looks nice, they seem to be really expensive.

The first few times I went to buy a bra and get fitted I was incredibly shy and scared. I didn't want anyone seeing. Now I've just got used to it. I remember one older bra fitter said to me, 'You're only 14! Your boobs are very big!' At that point, I thought it was quite funny, but if I had been younger I would have been mortified and upset. By then, I could deal with it.

I did notice that people looked at me differently when I was not in an all-girls environment and I was around boys,

NEWSFLASH
Whatever you are experiencing, you won't be the only person to feel like that. No one feels like they are normal.

especially Year 7 and Year 8 time. I remember coming home after an event once and I said to my mum, 'When all the boys talk to me, they just stare at my boobs'. But it's basically been fine. The main frustration is trying to shop at a normal high street shop. If the clothes are aimed at people my age, then styles often don't work. They can look inappropriate because the style isn't expecting you to have larger breasts. If I wear something that looks normal on someone else, it can look too revealing on me. When you are younger, you don't want to be pushed into wearing clothes that are too revealing and show too much. You don't want to be labelled just because of the clothes you wear. You don't feel ready to think about yourself as 'sexy' when you are 14 or 15 but other people are sometimes doing it to you.

I'm lucky because my mum is very, 'boobs are normal. Boobs are about breastfeeding. The most important thing is not what your boobs look like'. I think that has been a really good influence. In an all-girls school I also feel like it's been a good environment as there's less focus on your body. I'm really fine with how I look. Sometimes I'm just frustrated that the rest of the world doesn't catch up and realise larger boobs are normal. Clothes need to be designed differently. They are missing out on a big chunk of the market.

Social media does affect teenage girls, but teenage girls are also able to recognise when something isn't real and is artificial and marketed. We've caught on more than older people realise to understand that social media isn't necessarily the real world and people are often trying to sell you something.

I'd say to a young girl just starting to develop that everyone around you feels self-conscious, no matter what stage they are at. Whatever you are experiencing, you won't be the only person to feel like that. No one feels like they are normal. If you feel self-conscious, talk to your friends. Everyone will be relieved that someone else feels the same way.

CHAPTER SEVEN

Our breast friends

We've already heard from lots of people about their lives with their breasts: their memories of how they first grow, buying a first bra, how developing can sometimes be an uncomfortable experience and what it's like to use breasts for feeding babies.

Next are some longer stories from Vanisha, Somaiya, Philippa, Zainab and Iyato. Their stories are all very different but you'll notice some things are the same. You'll notice how worrying about being normal can bring a lot of anxiety and finding people to talk to and not worrying alone helps everyone. Sometimes the people who help aren't always who you might expect. It may take time before someone feels comfortable inside their own body. Breastfeeding often transforms how a woman feels about her breasts and, even when it has been a struggle, it is something mums look back on with pride.

Vanisha, 41

My mum brought me up quite liberal. Naked bodies everywhere. Nothing in our family was taboo, we could talk about anything.

Despite that, my first memory of breasts is a negative one.

I remember around the age of 11, we went on a camping trip to Great Yarmouth. It was my first trip without my mum. My cousin and my sister (we were all around the same age) sometimes used to pick on me. I was always studious and reading in the corner. I remember on the minibus, my sister and my cousin tried to get a rise out of me. They made up a song about me. The song was about 'Vanisha and her one and a half breasts'. One was an A cup and one was a B cup. I remember the worker in the minibus was worried about how I was feeling, but I was fine. At least I had some breasts! Even then I knew it was normal to have one side a bit bigger than the other. I wasn't upset. I was more annoyed by everyone asking me how I was and thinking I *should* be upset. I was interested in looking out the window at the greenery and looking for cows!

My mum had the philosophy, 'if you don't know something look it up'. In those days it was the library and not the internet. I had self-confidence from being able to talk about things. Mum was originally from St Lucia in the Caribbean. She came over to England when she was 10. My dad came over from Jamaica when he was seven. We grew up in south London. My parents have been married for 41 years.

My mum breastfed us all for six months and then switched us to cups and beakers. My mum worked in the office in childcare and took us to the office. My mum got pregnant with my sister when I was very little and still breastfeeding. Maybe her milk dried up when she was pregnant so I didn't get as much.

At 16 years old, I was about a C cup. I was very active. Then I left school and I was less active and I'm now a nice juicy size.

After school, I went into catering but then I realised I wanted to work in childcare. I love it. It's a bit like gardening. You reap what you sow. You have to do the weeding and the discipline and give boundaries. But you can be loving and caring.

As I got older, it took me a while to find the right bra. You go by what everyone else tells you. I was wearing the wrong size – I didn't feel supported. I had a double boob. When I was fitted properly, the ache in the shoulders went and I stood up straighter and I felt more comfortable in my body. Having the right bra gave me a positive lease of life. I'm quite lucky. My breasts are quite perky. Bras help me feel confident. The right bra shop should give you practical advice and not just focus on trying to sell you something. Maybe the bra you already have just needs adjusting. Maybe the straps need shortening or something.

When I was younger, my mum was working in a project where the police work with the community. I remember the police giving us a few tips to look after ourselves. We were taught to speak out, know your body is yours. Stand straight, walk confidently. I'm trying to think if there's ever a time when my breasts got me unwanted attention? I can remember when I was about 18 and my aunt had a new husband and I met him at a barbeque. By then I had big breasts and he was looking at me a certain way. I always had a bit of a mouth on me and I looked at him and said, 'This is not your dinner'. He was looking at me like I was a plate of food. I said, 'YOU need to go and get some food'. My mum brought up four strong women. We are all no-nonsense and stand up for ourselves.

I had Micah when I was 39. I didn't have much support if I'm honest. I was a single mum. My friend Donna was with me in the hospital. When Micah was first born, he was unresponsive. I didn't see Micah for several hours when he was born. He was in neonatal for five days. He had breathing difficulties and a slow pulse rate.

The nurse asked if I wanted to breast or bottle feed and I thought I would try breastfeeding. When I was pregnant, I just thought about feeding him. I knew some of the health benefits of breastfeeding and I thought it might be nice to try, but I just wanted to feed him. I'd worked in childcare and I'd worked with bottle-fed and breastfed babies. I knew breastfeeding would be better for him because we had allergies in the family, but it wasn't down to me, it was down to him. They put him on and he went straight on. He knew what to do.

I'm still breastfeeding Micah. My dad is fine with it. My mum sometimes says to him, 'you're a big boy now'. Like he should stop. I say to her, 'You're a 60-something-year-old woman and you drink the breastmilk of a cow. When you wean, talk to me about weaning'. She knows about the health implications. He has allergies and it's really helped with his eczema. At the end of the day, it's our breasts, our business. He was never interested in the bottle. That's fine with me. It's easier. At three o'clock in the morning, I just roll over and it's there.

I trained as a breastfeeding supporter because I didn't have any support. I remember the woman beside me in hospital wanted to breastfeed but she couldn't get the right help. Her bed was beside mine. I'm still in touch with her. Even two years later, she is upset that her breastfeeding journey never really began. They gave her formula milk and a cup and they didn't help her. Another woman in a bed near me saw me feeding Micah and asked me to breastfeed her baby. I would have if I hadn't been taking a lot of medication. She wasn't getting support either. The hospital was really busy.

I'm quite lucky because where I live a lot of people breastfeed. Not so much in the part of London where my mum lives. Most of my family didn't breastfed or didn't attempt to.

Sometimes the studies say that black women are more likely to breastfeed, but you can't generalise about any community. African mums are more likely to breastfeed in my experience. Often they are in touch with their cultural background and connected to grandparents who breastfed. In my experience, women from the Caribbean, not so much. In the Caribbean, the formula companies do a lot of advertising. There are billboards everywhere. Cheap formula milk comes from America.

Breastfeeding a toddler is not easy. They try and breastfeed while they watch telly and do acrobatics. It's not comfortable. I'm lucky he's not bitten me, but when a new tooth comes through, it takes him a while to figure things out. Once he sneezed and I screamed the house down. I'm aware I'm raising a young prince. I want him to respect women and all shapes and sizes. I want him to uplift a woman and make his queen feel like a queen. I want him to have a positive image of women.

Love your breasts. Touch them and feel them and know what they are supposed to look and feel like. They will grow and change. If you know them, you'll know if there are ever any health problems. Love them. Because if you don't love them, how can anyone else love them?!

Somaiya, 33

My family originally came from India. I was born in England, but we moved around a lot: Bahrain, Cairo, Dubai.

I'm the eldest of six children and when I was growing up, my mum was focused on being a mother.

I remember my mum breastfeeding. She was very private about it. She breastfed my youngest brother Ebi (who's now 12) until he was two. The rest of us for just a few months. She told me she gave me formula milk very early on because that was the done thing. When she breastfed my youngest brother, because she was so religious, she breastfed him mainly on the right breast because the right side was 'favoured' by God. She ended up being a bit lop-sided, but that's what she thought was the right thing to do. In the Qu'ran (the holy book of Islam), it says the prophet Muhammad was breastfed on the right side by his wet nurse. I pointed out to her that this was probably because the wet nurse was feeding her own baby on the left, which she agreed was maybe true!

When I saw my mum breastfeed, I didn't think she was doing anything special. But now I look back I think about her breastfeeding Ebi until he was two, when she was an older mum, and I think, 'Well done, mum!'

I was quite young when my breasts started to develop. My mum was really unhelpful, and I don't mind telling you that. She told me about periods and told me I had to hide it all – my period and my breasts. If I was in pain, I always had to stand up straight. She said that when I bought a bra, I always had to be measured over my clothes. But she does have a younger sister who is a bit of a free-thinker. She took me for my first bra fitting. I remember I bought a white one, a beige one and a navy one. The navy one was so pretty, it was almost too special to wear. I just looked at it. It was so beautiful. I felt proud of my three bras, but also unable to ask my mum for help, which is a shame looking back. I'm sure she was the same with my sisters, but by then I had figured things out, so I made sure that they had proper bra fittings and we had a trip to the shops together. For them it was a rite of passage and hopefully a positive experience. For me, it was something I had to 'deal with' and 'hide'.

I always worried about the shape of my breasts. Even in cartoons, breasts always seem perky and round. But actually, breasts are a tear-drop shape. When I was younger I thought I might even need an operation when I was older. That's so bad. Why did I think that? I thought there was something wrong with them! They weren't exactly the same size. I didn't have cleavage and they were too far apart. I had a very dark areola. Did other women have areolae that dark? I'm very tan and of course the colour of my skin would mean a darker areola. I was very curious about whether I was normal but there was no one to ask.

I wish I knew that just like our faces – which come in all sorts of beautiful shapes and sizes, sometimes symmetrical and sometimes not – our breasts are not symmetrical. There is a beauty in things that aren't symmetrical. I have a mole on one side of my face and one on one breast. Those are MY breasts. If there were a picture of a row of breasts, I'd know which ones were mine! Breasts change throughout your life. They get heavier and change when you put on weight or lose weight and when you get pregnant. If you get pregnant, they are amazing things.

I also wish I'd known that breasts can get sore around your period. That's normal. No one told me that. Sometimes one side and not the other. That made me really anxious when I was younger. I thought maybe that meant one side would be huge.

It can be awkward to be an early developer and be one of the first. I remember at the end of Year 5, it was a hot day and when I lifted my arms up in class, people saw the hair under my arm. I was the first one to have any. Everyone, including the teacher, was surprised. I remember being mortified! I wish someone had told me that might happen. I didn't even notice the hair was there! Nobody even told me to expect hair near my private parts. I remember getting a shock when I was reading in the bath one day and looked down. Remember there's always someone to talk to – an aunt, an older friend – if not your mum. It's good to talk together as girls. I remember being the first one to wear a bra and agonising over whether it could be seen under my white shirt. I was living in Bahrain in the Middle East where it was really hot, but I had a vest over my bra and my shirt as well. My mum always said it mustn't be seen.

Girls are so lucky today. They have special pants you can wear during your period and bras made of modern technology – comfortable fabrics and lots of choice and you don't have to have wires that cut into you.

My sister Baraka was diagnosed with lung cancer when she was 22 and I took a sabbatical (a break) from work to care for her and help support her through her treatment. She died soon after I became pregnant with my son Zaki and one of the last things I was able to tell her was that I was expecting a baby. I'm so glad I took that time out to be with her. My sister Baraka (which means blessing) was spiritual. Her faith gave her a sense of peace and a strength to face death. She had an acceptance.

It was a bit cheeky because I came home and just told my husband that I was giving up work to look after her and he was amazing and so supportive. She came to live with us because we were near the hospital where she was being treated and we ate together and supported her through her chemotherapy (when you don't always feel like eating). She told me to go back to work after she died and I did. I worked and I was pregnant so I had to eat and carry on. I had a feeling of awful emptiness and ache, but going back to work saved me in a way. Life goes on.

My husband Nicholas is Swiss-French and adopted. His mum is a nurse and his dad was a psychiatrist. Zaki, his baby son, was the first time he ever saw and met his own blood relative. Now I'm a mum, I really feel for my own parents when I think about them losing my sister. It's hard to lose a sibling, but I cannot imagine losing a child you have raised. I have had a miscarriage but I can't imagine losing a child in the way they did.

My parents are very religious and that's their way of coping. Everyone has their own way of showing grief. Their religion gives them a sense that they will meet my sister again. And maybe that losing her was God's will (although that's difficult for me to square).

They do mind that I'm not religious. I used to wear a hijab (a head covering) and when I was about 20, I said to them, 'I can't do this anymore. I'm not doing it for the right reasons. I'm not sure what I believe'. That was painful for them. I told them I couldn't wear it to please other people. They are hurt that I don't pray with them because that was something the family did together.

When I was pregnant, I just assumed I would breastfeed. I thought it would be easier. I thought it would naturally happen. I remember seeing my aunts breastfeed when I was younger and the babies looked so happy. The women in the family were all together chatting and breastfeeding and there wasn't any awkwardness. I knew that's how babies were fed.

When I had Zaki, I didn't realise how hard it could be. He was about a month early and I just wasn't ready. I remember my mum came to the hospital and I said to her, 'How do I hold him? How did you do this?' She said if it got too hard I could just switch to a bottle but I was really keen to breastfeed. I'd read it up on how it was good for the baby. I got there in the end with lots of help from lactation consultants and midwives and my husband too being very patient and supporting me through all the anxiety.

I remember on the way home from hospital, it was raining. My husband was driving us in the car and I was crying and the baby was crying. When we got home, I remember getting ready to give him a bottle because he hadn't been latching on the breast properly and my mother-in-law was there, and she suggested I just try and breastfeed. My mother-in-law had adopted all three of her children and she hadn't had experience of breastfeeding, but she's a really firm believer that it's the best thing you can do for your child if you can do it. She said, 'just try'. He got on and he fed! Then it got easier. I started to enjoy it.

Later on, I went to a breastfeeding group to meet other mums who were breastfeeding. When he was three months old, Zaki was so fat. I felt a great sense of accomplishment because I had done that. He hadn't eaten anything else! That was my milk that made that beautiful fat baby! This is a world that measures everything. We know about the calories in an apple. With breastfeeding, you have to 'believe' that he's having enough. At the beginning there was constant questioning – he had seven minutes and three minutes and fell asleep. Should I wake him up? Am I doing the right thing? In the end, it got easier and I decided to let him lead.

My son Zaki is now 17 months. He's a big baby and people often think he's older. I did go back to work for a while. Zaki was in nursery two days a week and I went back to work in finance (I'd been a journalist before that) but he never settled. The nursery said that at 12 months he was unhappy 60% of the time. I didn't feel I could do that to him. I handed in my resignation. Perhaps if he'd started nursery as a smaller baby it would have been easier.

Initially, feeding outside the home was really difficult. You spend all your life covering up and breasts are taboo. I started using a cover like an apron when I was breastfeeding outside the home, but Zaki hates being covered up. He doesn't like heavy things on his legs. He didn't like being under things. I started putting his needs ahead of mine. It felt fine. I was a bit anxious the first time, but I realised if people don't like it, they can look away. By the time I'd find a private corner, he would have been screaming. It felt natural even though my whole life had been about modesty. I'd even worn a hijab and now I'm breastfeeding out and about. I never really had negative feedback for feeding in public. Just one time, I was in a park. Zaki was upset. He'd had a tumble or something – you don't just feed for food but for comfort too. And a man walked past when I was feeding and rolled his eyes. It didn't matter to me at all. It said more about him than it did about me.

There are so many things I am proud of having accomplished in my life professionally and personally, but I really feel that satisfying my baby's needs when he is hungry or needs comfort – and the only person he can get it from is me –

is the most wonderful feeling of contentment and satisfaction I have ever had.

At the children's centre one day, someone suggested I train to support other mums. I trained as a breastfeeding peer supporter. Zaki would sleep in the sling and I went along to the training. I don't come from a medical background although I nursed my sister when she was ill. Maybe in another life I would have done something medical. I'm amazed by what women can do and I think breastfeeding is just so fantastic. I passionately wanted to volunteer.

I don't have any intention to stop breastfeeding Zaki, but people have asked me ever since he turned one, 'When are you going to stop?'. Even my mother-in-law, who was such a great support at the beginning and would bring me a cup of tea when I was feeding in the middle of the night. Even she says that 'I'm not helping him to be independent'. That doesn't make sense to me. I don't think it stops them being independent or makes them think unhealthily about breasts. My friend's son, who stopped breastfeeding when he was three, went to the National Gallery with his class at school. As they went through the Renaissance gallery with paintings of naked women and cherubs flying around, his friends were sniggering, and he was just, 'What's the big deal? The women are just feeding those flying fat babies!'. I'm going to do my own thing. Which is what's got me to here. I think my mother-in-law will understand. I've been really lucky with my family. My family I've married into and the one I have.

When you are younger, it's easy to feel disempowered by the changes that are happening to you; your skin may break out, your breasts may hurt as they grow or when you get your period, you will get hair in unexpected places. I would find a friend you can talk to – if you cannot speak to your mum try a peer in your year, a teacher, a cousin or an aunt... Half the world's population have gone through or will go through these changes – so you should know you are not alone! Some manage these changes with grace, many don't. I look back years later and recall the anxiety, the humiliation and mortification I felt so keenly, and now I'm able to laugh at the absurdity of it, although at the time I really suffered alone and in silence.

Worrying about how I had one breast bigger than the other, being one of the first to hit puberty, crippling pain during my periods and not being able to talk about it because of the social stigma – I was definitely not an enviable teenager with fantastic hair and skin, but rather I was socially awkward and constantly embarrassed by what my body was going through and trying to mask growing changes with bad posture. All these outward changes to our bodies take place when we start to feel so much inwardly too. I wish I had known that ultimately the sum of what makes us is so much greater than what we look like.

Of all the women I have known from my mother to my younger sister, my aunts and my friends – the ones who are happiest seem to be those who accept that at a basic level you cannot control how you look beyond eating healthily and exercising. Don't be ashamed or disgusted by changes that you cannot control, instead try to enjoy the gift that is your body and celebrate all the incredible things that you are capable of. Our bodies are constantly evolving from the moment we are conceived right the way through life. Change is inevitable and if you can embrace it you'll find self-confidence, which I was certainly missing in my youth.

Philippa, 29

I was born the youngest of seven children – five girls and two boys. I was born totally blind, which was a bit of a shock to my parents, but I did everything that my brothers and sisters did. I had chores around the house. I went to mainstream school all the way through. When I left school, I worked for an auction centre on the telephone switchboard. Then I started working for a charity called Through the Roof, which helps disabled people to live normal lives and helps churches and organisations to include disabled people. I went on mission trips with them to Guatemala in South America.

I met my husband on holiday in 2012. Got married in 2013. Now I have two children – both girls. One is three and a half years old and one is 13 months old. My husband is also blind. He was given too much oxygen when he was born premature and it damaged his eyes.

My first memories of breasts were my mum being teased because she had quite big boobs. People used to say my sister was going to be the same. People used to laugh and joke. Some people apparently had breasts like 'fried eggs' and some people had big boobs. If you're blind, you don't see boobs and you don't go around feeling them, but you can hear people talking about them. I assumed one day I'd have big boobs like mum. When I was about 12 or 13, I started developing a bit and I got my first bra. I think it was a hand-me-down. I wore it because that's what people did and it made me feel grown-up. I didn't need to wear it though. By 16, I still didn't have all that much. I wasn't that worried. I was still at school. I wasn't really thinking much about boyfriends.

I started to feel like I wasn't very attractive and I was worried about my breasts. I kept hearing people talk about 'big boobs'. I knew mine weren't, because the cup of the bra was always really baggy and I would fill out the bottom of the cup but not the top. I had to stuff bras with tissues. I ended up going to talk to my doctor when I was about 21.

I said, 'Listen, I don't know if I really have a problem. I might be imagining things. I might be barking up the wrong tree. Can you look at my breasts and tell me if they are normal or not?' My doctor said, 'actually, I can see what you mean'. And he listened to me. It was a relief that he agreed. It felt really empowering. My breasts were like tubes. I had big nipples that were quite fat but not much else. They were like empty tubes with a nipple at the end. And there was a massive gap between the tubes. He went away and did some research and found out that I could have some surgery on the NHS.

I told the doctors that if I had surgery I wanted them to know that I wanted to breastfeed one day. In the surgery, they put an implant under my muscle – a bag of salty water. They didn't put all the water in the bag in straight away. They did it in gradual stages. They put a valve under my arm and then they could gradually add more water with injections to give my breast skin a chance to stretch. I was 23 when I had the surgery. The operation wasn't easy. I was rushed back in because I had a bleed. The surgery was quite sore and the inside of my breasts itched and I felt the stretching. But after the operation, it made such a difference. I was able to buy a bra and fit it properly. My shape isn't completely 'cured'. They are still a bit of a funny shape but my confidence was so much better.

No one ever told me what had been wrong with me. It was only after my surgery, when I was in the hospital ward in bed and the doctor came in with some students, and he pulled the curtains from around my bed and I heard him say, 'This is the woman with tubular breast syndrome'. No one had ever said that to me before.

I got married in my new wedding dress with my new boobs. I knew when I had children I wanted to breastfeed. Everyone in my family had breastfed. My sister had breastfed her two sets of twins and her two other children. My mum breastfed me for 18 months, which wasn't always easy for her because I couldn't see what was happening and I was pushing her away. Breastfeeding in my family was open and that was what was normal. In my family, there are 28 nieces and nephews and six great nieces and nephews, and everyone has at least started out breastfeeding.

When I was pregnant, I told my midwife about my implant surgery and she said it didn't matter. I told the health visitor too so everybody knew. I even told THEM I had this thing called tubular breast syndrome but they didn't seem to know what that might mean. No one explained to me that my tubular breast syndrome might make it difficult for me to make enough milk for my baby.

"A new breastfeeding lady who was trained by Baby Friendly was kinder. She explained that any milk I could make would be valuable, but my baby needed extra milk."

When my daughter was born, I put her on the breast straight away and she seemed to be feeding. She was quite sleepy and would fall asleep quickly after five minutes. I knew babies fed a lot so I wasn't worried. But by day seven, she stopped doing poos. She didn't poo for nine days and she was putting on weight slowly. Different people came to my house but it felt like they weren't explaining things. No one had told me in pregnancy I might not make enough milk for my baby. If they had, it might have all felt very different. Not everyone was very nice. One health visitor said I was 'starving' my baby. My in-laws said I was being selfish for wanting to breastfeed. It felt like they were telling me that what I wanted to do for my baby was worthless. A new breastfeeding lady who was trained by Baby Friendly was kinder. She explained that any milk I could make would be valuable, but my baby needed extra milk. She talked about pumping to help my milk supply. I got into a routine of breastfeeding, giving baby a bottle and pumping. I hired a great big breast pump.

I took some herbs to help my milk supply. I worked hard with the pumping. I did lots of skin-to-skin. I got an SNS (supplementary nursing system), which saved my feeding relationship. It's a thin tube you can use at the breast to give baby extra milk while they are still on the breast. All the extra milk was given at the breast rather than with a bottle; that made me feel better. The Baby Friendly breastfeeding counsellor explained it wasn't the surgery that had made a difference, but what my breasts had been like before. After five months, someone finally told me that it might have been my tubular breasts and I had something called 'insufficient glandular tissue'. I was gutted. If they had known about it, why wasn't I told? Then I got pregnant again and I stopped breastfeeding.

I lost two babies but then my second daughter was born. I did lots of research when I was pregnant. I learnt about drugs that might help my milk supply. I got in contact with a lactation consultant. I talked to lots of people. I got my breast pump sorted. I expressed some colostrum when I was pregnant. I thought I might produce a bit more second time around.

My second daughter breastfed straight away but she also got sleepy quickly. I pumped after every feed. I spoke to the lactation consultant. I used the tube. I was still having to give formula as well as my milk.

I was still beating myself up, even though I knew it might happen again. I felt like it was my fault. I was INSUFFICIENT. It felt like I didn't just have insufficient glandular tissue, but I was also an insufficient mother. I kept getting different midwives who thought my breasts looked normal and I should have enough milk. I kept having to tell them that I knew I had a medical condition. I knew I had to give my daughter extra milk or she would die. And the midwives were saying, 'Your breasts look normal. You should have plenty of milk', and I was saying, 'What PLANET do you live on?'. I just carried on doing what I needed to do. I carried on pumping. I was getting a bit more milk. But I kept feeling awful and blaming myself. I had lots of anxiety. I didn't mind feeding in public but I minded using the tube feeding system in public because someone might ask me questions. I didn't want my in-laws to see and I'd feed her in a different room when they were around. I used to hide it. I didn't want people to see in public that I wasn't enough and I needed to give extra milk.

I got over that bit in the end. Now I can go to groups and if she needs extra milk in public, I can give it to her. I realise now if people did see, they wouldn't mind. I think I wanted to prove a point to myself. It stems from being blind and people assume you won't be able to do certain things. I needed to prove something.

After a while, I started to notice that my baby was reacting badly to the formula. She was upset and uncomfortable. She had funny poo. I thought she might have dairy allergies. A doctor gave me a different formula in which the dairy proteins were changed to stop the baby reacting to them. I also got a drug that helped me to make more milk. I had to go back to using a bottle because the special milk was too thick to be used with the tube at the breast. I loathed having to pack formula. It felt so unfair. I didn't give a toss about being blind, but I hated not being able to breastfeed her. When I made formula bottles, I felt like a part of me was dying. I was always worried I would get it wrong when I made up formula even though part of me knew I could do it and I hadn't made mistakes before. I also started to use more milk donated from other mums. The human milk agreed with her much better. People sent me the milk they had in their freezer. She had loads of breastmilk and she was so much better.

Eventually at about seven months, things started to settle. I got into a groove of using formula sometimes but then feeding her whenever I wanted. She still wanted me through everything. Sometimes she'd come back to me straight after a bottle. It really helped me. If she falls over, she comes over to me and wants to feed at the breast. If she's upset, she comes over and wants a feed. So, my boobs can't do everything, but they are pretty awesome. She thinks they are awesome. Through everything, she's always wanted to come to the breast. I'd always hated my boobs. What was the point in them? But she had made me feel better about them. She wants them!

I would say to anyone who is worried about their breasts

or their feeding, don't let anyone fob you off. The size of your breasts might not matter, but the shape can. Talk to your GP or a lactation consultant if you are worried.

Now I want to make sure mums get the support they need. I've trained as a breastfeeding volunteer to help other mums and I'm hoping there will be ways I can educate others about what happened to me, like writing an article and talking to healthcare professionals. I'd like to help all mums who need it, but also specialise in helping mums with insufficient glandular tissue. I'm a volunteer with Blind Mums Connect, but I support new mums with lots of different aspects of new parenthood. I feel like my story happened to me for a reason. I need to make sure that what happened to me had a purpose.

Zainab, 36

I don't have a lot of memories from when I was younger, but I know my mum breastfed all seven of us. I was born in Iran and we came to England when I was quite young. My mum is Iranian, and my dad is English. When I was younger, I got polio and it affected my leg, so I spent a lot of time in hospital. I had a lot of surgeries. Sometimes, I went to school in hospital and I sometimes stayed for months and I was in hospital when some of my younger siblings were born.

Breastfeeding and periods weren't really talked about when I was growing up. No one talked to me about periods as far as I remember. I made a decision that when my younger sister grew up, she would have me to talk to. I remember she once came to talk to me about shaving and I explained to her that when you start shaving, you change your hair forever. Before you shave, your hair is soft and wispy and once you shave it grows back thicker, darker and more noticeable. I wish I'd never started shaving! You keep having to do it and your skin gets sore and dry. It's such a hassle. Your skin gets aggravated and irritated. NO one tells you that. Luckily now, young women are hearing more about how they don't have to shave.

Later on, my parents got divorced and I went away to university. My family moved to north London. I continued studying at university and did further academic study while I was working in public health and I got married.

When I was pregnant, I knew I was going to breastfeed. Religiously (we were Muslim), you always knew that you would breastfeed until your baby was two. That was what was going to happen. When my first baby was born, I fed him within about an hour of him being born. I remember being a new mum was quite a shock. I looked at my engorged full breasts and I couldn't believe how big they were! It didn't seem possible for my body to get that big. Everything was very painful in the beginning. Being a new mum wasn't easy. I saw a breastfeeding counsellor after about five weeks and a health visitor who helped me. My husband told me that my positioning at the breast had looked a bit off, but I couldn't believe it was something as easy as positioning. But the breastfeeding supporters told me the same thing.

But even when the latch was better, I struggled with the frequency of breastfeeding. After about three and a half months, it started to get to me. I didn't know many people who were going through what I was going through. Motherhood was overwhelming. I struggled with the feeling that my body wasn't mine and my body had changed. I can't pinpoint one thing, but it was hard. When he started solid food, he didn't eat much and wanted the breast more. I hadn't expected that. That was another big adjustment. It felt like he was constantly on there. Maybe he could sense I was struggling to adjust to new motherhood? I don't know.

I got pregnant again when my first son was just under two. I didn't know I was pregnant at first. I got really tired.

I continued to find breastfeeding hard. I had to distract myself to be able to cope. I wanted to carry on breastfeeding and offer him the nourishment and support and love and contact. But at the same time, I completely couldn't bear him being latched on. Both feelings happened simultaneously. When he was breastfeeding, I would get agitated and upset. I would let him latch and I wanted to give him milk but I would feel like taking him off at the exact same time.

It would sometimes be easier. Sometimes I would distract myself and it wasn't so bad. Part of the problem is I am a busybody. I found it really hard to sit down. I'm someone who likes to potter around and get things done. Having to sit down for a long time was difficult. I thought I was the only one feeling like this – the only one who wanted to breastfeed while also finding it really uncomfortable and upsetting at the same time. I didn't feel in control of my own body. Growing up, I had learnt to be in control of my own body. We were feisty when we were girls. If we didn't want someone touching us – if we didn't want a boy touching us – we might hit them! But now, I had to give my body up to someone and I didn't own my own body. My son needed it.

I didn't tell many people how I was feeling. At first my husband couldn't understand why I didn't love breastfeeding but later he was an important support in helping by distracting me. Some friends just thought I should stop breastfeeding. They were confused about why I would want to continue.

When I had my second child, I started to write about my

experience of how I felt during breastfeeding. I posted on social media and people started sharing their stories, which were similar to mine. I wasn't the only one to want to breastfeed even though I found it hard.

If someone is finding breastfeeding upsetting, it's always good to start by going to a breastfeeding support group. There may be practical things that can help, like looking at how the baby is latched on. It can also help to know what's normal. Women can feel angry and frustrated if their expectation doesn't match the reality. Maybe if people know that frequent breastfeeding can be normal, they will feel less of that frustration. Joining support groups online can help too. It can be helpful to be able to say that you hate breastfeeding (even if you still want to do it!) and express your feelings. Sometimes taking certain dietary supplements like magnesium and vitamin B12 supplements can help. When your baby is older, it might help to reduce how often the baby is feeding at night or put in some restrictions.

Now I've finished breastfeeding both my children and I can look back. It was a very, very special part of my life. It completely changed me. It was really difficult, but I really wanted to do it. It was my greatest achievement and probably always will be. I felt proud of being able to say I gave them my milk. I'm not super health-conscious, but I know you are what you eat. I didn't want to give them formula. I just didn't want to. But I didn't expect them to be so dependent on me and my breasts.

When you start breastfeeding, you have emotions you weren't expecting. You build solidarity with other women. You find friendships. It's a whole world.

I used to hate my body. I wasn't comfortable with it. Then I found some body positive people and body positive conversations on social media and started to feel better about myself. Maybe it's because breasts are sexual things and shifting from that to them having another function was difficult. Maybe it's easier for them to be attractive to men than it is for them to have a function that is such hard work for the person who owns the breasts?

It can be hard for young girls when their body changes. I remember finding out that my friend had two differently sized breasts like I did and that was really comforting. When you are worried you aren't normal, it can take your world over. I don't think boys really care though! A man who would get to look at breasts wouldn't be bothered about them being different sizes!

Sometimes when we see women wearing certain clothing, we make assumptions about them. We might see someone with really small shorts and think she is being 'sexy', but maybe she wants to be comfortable and isn't focused on being sexy at all. I think sometimes when people see someone breastfeeding in public, they struggle with the real intentions of why a mum might be showing some skin. It's about feeding a baby, not trying to attract anyone. There's really no need to cover when you breastfeed and babies often don't like being under covers. It's just a pressure from society that you should be covered. But there's another pressure sometimes to NOT cover.

If I was talking to a young girl about her body changing, I would say that ANYTHING you feel, ANYTHING you are worried about, ANYTHING that is happening to you has happened to another person, or is happening to another person right now, or will happen to another person. You are not alone. Just find someone to talk to. Any concern you are having, will be happening to someone else. Find someone who has shared your experience.

Iyato, 30s

I wish society considered breasts – female breasts – like any other body part.

I wish society treated female breasts like male breasts – not a big deal, not a prop to sell products, not something to get overly excited about, hide, be very conscious of, thought of as a distraction, or used to justify treating females in favourable or unfavourable ways.

In so many ways, female breasts are 'not a big deal'; but when it comes to their biological function and primary purpose, they are a big deal! Breasts are the most effective, efficient, and sustainable way of keeping new babies alive and thriving all around the world, for all time.

My first memory of 'breasts' is probably my dad's. I remember him going into his room after coming home from work and coming back to the sitting room shirtless or wearing a loose singlet. His breasts were sizeable compared to some of the other shirtless men I saw growing up.

My first memory of my breasts was when I tried to breastfeed one of my younger brothers when he was a baby. I was holding my brother while sitting on a chair in our living room. Interestingly, I can't remember seeing any of my brothers being breastfed, but I assume I must have seen some breastfeeding to get the idea that breasts could feed or soothe a baby. I was around five years old when this happened.

I don't think I thought much about my breasts until they started growing. I wasn't quite like the other girls. I was the youngest in my classes because I was fast-tracked through the year groups in primary school. One of the consequences of this was that I appeared to go through puberty later than the other girls and I was very aware that my body wasn't quite as developed. Unfortunately, a few of my school mates were particularly unkind about this.

Puberty can be especially confusing, particularly if you don't have people around you to support you as you need. I didn't.

If I could go back in time to hang out with my 10-year-old self with what seemed like slowly developing breasts, I'll remind her about the joy she brought to so many hearts when she was born. I'll tell her that every way she has developed from the moment she was conceived has been a celebration. I'll also tell her that her developing breasts are wonderful; they show she's growing into a woman and that's good. Growing and maturing is a lovely part of the circle of life. Like babies learning to see and toddlers learning to walk, it can be a steep learning curve.

I will also tell her she might have a range of emotions about it, in figuring out how this fits with her body as she has known it so far, and other people's interaction with her because of it; it's all very normal.

'Be kind to yourself, girl', I'll tell her, 'and don't worry about how long it takes, what the size is, or how it looks; our bodies are unique to us and that's okay'. I'll tell her that she has got this, as she got her eyes, ears, legs, lungs, and much more.

Furthermore, I'll encourage her to learn more about the incredible and mind-blowing primary function of female breasts, to support them with comfy bras when needed, to treat them with respect like the rest of her body, and to enjoy them. Lastly, I'll tell her to talk with those she trusts and feels comfortable with on that level and to write about it in her journal if she wants.

Breastfeeding was the best thing that ever happened to my breasts and being a mum for me wouldn't be what it is without breastfeeding.

I found it very hard at the start. This was because I didn't educate myself about it before I had my baby. I just about made it to the NHS breastfeeding class, and while I listened and made notes, I didn't take it seriously enough and I didn't remember much of what was said afterwards.

I found it hard to accept that I couldn't fully feed my child from my breasts because of some of the challenges we had at the start, and some of the health professionals who helped me didn't seem to know enough about how breastmilk is produced. In the end, I spent a lot of time learning about how to make breastfeeding work and I worked hard on increasing my breastmilk supply until I could fully feed my baby myself.

I also learnt about how companies and society at large make breastfeeding harder than it should be, and I continue to learn about how amazing breastfeeding and breastmilk are. I have grown in confidence about what my breasts do, and I feel so empowered about meeting a lot of my children's needs through them. Breastfeeding has answered so many questions, known and unknown, for my children and me. We have learnt so much and grown together in ways that we wouldn't have without breastfeeding.

If I could, I would stop companies from selling their products with female breasts. I would also stop those that make breastmilk substitutes from competing against the primary function of breasts, and instead stick to stating facts about their products without lying about what they can do for the health of babies.

Breastfeeding showed me many things about the power of my breasts – the most self-sufficient, environmentally-sustainable,

and life-sustaining/thriving part of my body. It helped me to value my breasts. One of them is bigger than the other; the smaller one didn't produce much milk for several reasons. The amazing thing about this for me is that I've mainly used one breast over the last one and a half years to tandem breastfeed two children. This means that I breastfeed both my older and younger child. Occasionally I breastfeed them at the same time, but usually at different times. I can't get over how life-supporting my breasts are, even as my little ones get older and more independent of me. They give so much comfort to my children and me, they are a fast and quick pain relief, they help with sleep, and benefit our family in so many ways.

I don't care anymore about my breasts fitting into anyone's expectations about how to make them look presentable through my clothes. My breasts are for me and about me; they deserve comfy bras. I had this posh one as a teenager; a gift from a rich relative. I really liked that bra, and I used it for many years.

My breasts deserve respect for the incredible work they do for my children and me, my family and society at large.

If you'd like to read some more stories about breasts and see some photos, photographer and writer Laura Dodsworth's book *Bare Reality: 100 Women, Their Breasts, Their Stories* is a book that's not aimed at young people but you might find it interesting to look at with your grown-ups.

If something is really worrying you, and you don't know who you can talk to, you can always contact Childline by phoning 0800 1111 and they can help point you in the right direction. You can also chat online or send an email.

CHAPTER EIGHT

Your breast story

ou got to the end. Well done. How embarrassing was it on a scale of one to ten to read a book all about breasts?

Did you know people had so much to say about their milk and bras and breasts growing? Were you surprised that breasts could make people feel such a range of emotions? You'll have seen that breastfeeding is often very special for the people who have done it – something that they never forget, sometimes their proudest achievement, sometimes an experience that transformed how they appreciated their bodies. It doesn't always mean it's easy but then being a new mother isn't easy for anyone!

Take a look at your own chest. Where are you on the breast journey? I'm assuming you have nipples and areola. Any bumps on your areolae? Remember those are usually meant to be there, not spots you worry about.

Got any hairs? Also normal.

Your areola might be dark brown and nearly black. It might be pale brown. It might be dark pink or light pink. Areolae can be smaller (just the size of a small coin) or big (taking up a large portion of your breast). Your nipple might be sunk in slightly (inverted). It might stick out from your body quite a lot. It might be thin or wide. The other one might look completely different. Your nipple and areola might be on a mound away from your chest as they grow.

You might have one breast bigger than the other. You might not have any bump at all yet and you might be worried about that. You might have a lot of bump, and you might be worried about that.

Most of the time, you may not think about your breasts at all. They are a part of you and you've got lots of other things to worry about like being a friend, learning, expressing yourself, turning into the grown-up you want to be. One day you might be a parent. One day you might not. One day you might give your baby milk from your breast. Or you might not.

Whatever direction you go in, human breasts deserve a little bit of a celebration.

NEWSFLASH

The shape of your body is not the most important thing about you. How we think and behave and treat other people is the important bit. Be kind to others and be kind to yourself.

Things to remember:

1. Everyone's breasts are their own. They won't look exactly like anyone else's. They won't grow in the same way.
2. People usually worry that they are normal. If you are really worried, talk to someone. Being a human is easier when we share our feelings with other humans.
3. The shape of your body is not the most important thing about you. How we think and behave and treat other people is the important bit. Be kind to others and be kind to yourself.
4. You get to choose if you wear a bra. As you get older, you might feel that society bosses you around and tells you that you have to dress a certain way or look a certain way. Women throughout history have stood up to those pressures, and you can too.
5. Breasts are brilliant. Human milk is the perfect food for little humans. Scientists don't even understand all the things there are to know about human milk. They are learning more every day.
6. Breastfeeding isn't just about milk. It's about connecting emotionally, comfort, relaxation, helping sleep, building trust and relationships.
7. Whether or not you ever become a parent, help make a society where new parents feel welcome and supported. Feeding our babies shouldn't be hidden away. It's amazing!

Index

Acknowledgements

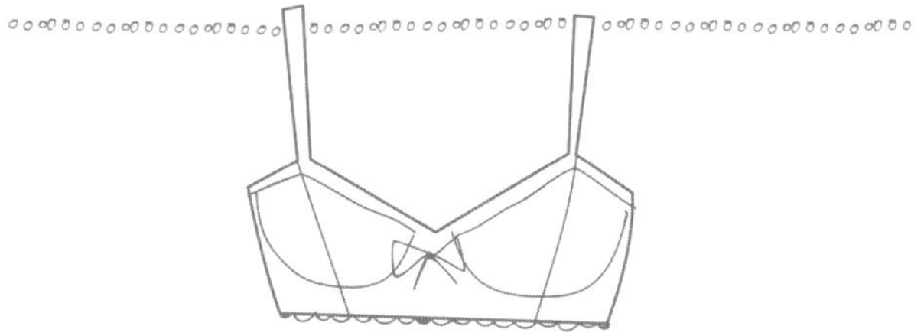

A special thank you to all the contributors who shared their experiences. It was an honour to hear your stories and journeys.

Thank you to the Association of Breastfeeding Mothers. This book wouldn't exist without you. Anyone who helps a new mum to meet her breastfeeding and infant feeding goals is my hero but you all have a special place in my heart.

Thank you to Agatha and Robert from RÅN studio and all the #feedme mums and babies for sharing your photos.

Thank you to the lovely team at Pinter & Martin, to Susan for saying this was an idea worth doing and to Allan and Fontaine for their work on the design and illustrations.

And thank you to J and S for being part of my breast story.